PRAISE FOR *BLACKBARN*

"What I find most impressive about John's extraordinary career is his mastery of cooking fundamentals, passionate embrace of seasonality, and the innovative twists he brings to each dish—all evident in the BLACKBARN cookbook, which is destined to be a future classic."
—Tim Ryan, president, Culinary Institute of America

"If experience counts, John Doherty is in the front rank. His peers consider him 'a chef's chef,' and his elegant new book shows his deep understanding of food and his impressive proficiency."
—John Mariani, The Virtual Gourmet

"The love of good food is what brings family and friends together. Eating seasonally, sourcing locally, and embracing the freshest ingredients is also something we believe in. That's what you'll find in the BLACKBARN cookbook."
—Steve Painter, executive chef and co-owner, The Log Cabin Restaurant

"BLACKBARN is more than a restaurant. It is a celebration of farm-to-table dining, warm hospitality, and the art of bringing people together. Chef John Doherty's culinary style blends rustic charm with contemporary sophistication. These recipes truly invite you to experience the magic of one of New York City's most beloved dining destinations—right from your kitchen."
—Chris O'Brien, executive chef and owner, Hyeholde Restaurant

"A terrific book! It captures the spirit and fun of seasonal eating and is packed with the recipes that made John and BLACKBARN famous."
—Neal Wavra, executive chef and owner, Field & Main Restaurant

JOHN DOHERTY

WITH
BRIAN FOWLER
ERIN HAYES

AND
JAMES O. FRAIOLI

BLACKBARN

RECIPES FROM OUR KITCHEN TO YOURS

NEW YORK

Skyhorse Publishing

Copyright © 2025 by John Doherty

Interior photography by Alan Batt (Battman Studios), Mark Zhelezoglo, Dillon Burke, Andrija Tadejevic, Melisa Hom, and Shutterstock.

All rights reserved. No part of this book may be reproduced in any manner without the express written consent of the publisher, except in the case of brief excerpts in critical reviews or articles. All inquiries should be addressed to Skyhorse Publishing, 307 West 36th Street, 11th Floor, New York, NY 10018.

Skyhorse Publishing books may be purchased in bulk at special discounts for sales promotion, corporate gifts, fund-raising, or educational purposes. Special editions can also be created to specifications. For details, contact the Special Sales Department, Skyhorse Publishing, 307 West 36th Street, 11th Floor, New York, NY 10018 or info@skyhorsepublishing.com.

Skyhorse® and Skyhorse Publishing® are registered trademarks of Skyhorse Publishing, Inc.®, a Delaware corporation.

Visit our website at www.skyhorsepublishing.com.

Culinary Book Creations LLC
www.culinarybookcreations.com

10 9 8 7 6 5 4 3 2 1

Library of Congress Cataloging-in-Publication Data on file.

Cover design by *the*BookDesigners
Cover photography by Battman

Hardcover ISBN: 978-1-5107-8419-2
Ebook ISBN: 978-1-5107-8438-3

Printed in China

DEDICATION

To all of those who helped my dream come true . . . my wife Jennifer, my business partner Tom, the dedicated staff, from our opening until now, and every guest who has walked through the door at BLACKBARN.

CONTENTS

Preface by Tom Struzzieri 14

My Culinary Journey by Chef John Doherty 16

Ingredients and Pantry 36

How to Use this Book to Eat and Drink through the Seasons 48

Tools and Equipment 52

Cooking Techniques 56

Essential Knife Cuts 68

MEET OUR CHEFS

Chefs Brian Fowler and Israel Reyes 74

Chef Marcos Castro and Pastry Chef Kerry Hegarty 77

BRUNCH

JUICES AND BEVERAGES 82

Carrot Mixer 84

Beetroot Juice 84

Green Juice 84

Bloody Mary with Homemade Hot Sauce 90

BREAKFAST PASTRIES 94

Almond Honey Croissant with Local Honey and Pear-Ginger Jam 96

Caramelized Croissant with Espresso Pastry Cream 100

Orange Cardamom Cinnamon Buns 102

APPETIZERS 106

Avocado Toast with Lemon Dressing 108

Charred Gem Lettuce with Green Goddess Dressing .112

Blue Corn "Johnny Cakes" 114

Maine Lobster Roll with Chimichurri Aioli and Roasted Tomatoes 116

MAINS 120

Corn Flake Crusted French Toast with Caramelized Apples and Crème Anglaise 122

Waffle Croque Madame with Cheese Fondue 126

Chorizo Egg and Cheese Empanada 130

BLACKBARN Burger with Homemade Cheese Brioche 134

EVENTS

SIGNATURE COCKTAILS 144

  Cloud 9 148

  Barnyard Tea 150

  Blushing Basil 152

HORS D'OEUVRES 154

  Gougères 156

  Vichyssoise with Homemade Chicken Stock 158

  Crispy Chicken Wings with Chipotle-Orange Spice Rub 162

  Mushroom Toast 164

MEET OUR SOMMELIER

  Andrija Tadejevic 168

SPRING

GARDEN 172

  White Asparagus with Morel Mushrooms and Buttermilk Dressing . . . 172

  Ricotta Zeppole with Preserved Tomato and White Bean Purée . . . 176

  Roasted Heirloom Carrots with English Pea Hummus 180

OCEAN 184

  Crab Cakes with Spinach-Ramp Purée 184

  Pan-Seared Day Boat Scallops with Crispy Pancetta and

  English Pea Risotto 188

PASTURE 192

  Bone Marrow with Manila Clams and Shallot Reduction 192

  Lamb Two Ways with Stuffed Zucchini Flower 196

  IPA Braised Cheshire Pork Shank with Charred Tomatillo Relish . . . 198

SIDES 202

  Shishito Peppers 202

  Crispy Anna Potatoes 204

DESSERT 206

  Chocolate Soufflé 206

  Roasted Figs and Almond Shortbread with Whipped Ricotta . . . 210

SUMMER

GARDEN 214

Grilled Corn and Kale Salad with Pickled Jalapeños 214

Watermelon Salad with Blue Cheese Dressing and Bermuda Onions 218

OCEAN 220

Bigeye Tuna Tartare 220

Butter Poached Maine Lobster with Fresh Pea Soup 224

Roasted Branzino with Spiced Roasted Carrots and Pan Roasted Potatoes 226

Polenta Cake with Ratatouille and Marinated Shrimp 230

PASTURE 236

Grilled Amish Chicken with Chimichurri and Panzanella Salad 236

BLACKBARN Tomahawk with Herb Butter 240

SIDES 244

Sautéed Zucchini with Garlic Crumbs 244

Roasted Peaches in White Bordeaux 246

DESSERT 248

Pavlova with Summer Fruit 248

Summer Berry Zabaglione with Lemon Lady Fingers 252

AUTUMN

GARDEN 256

Black Mission Fig Pizza 256

Cuban-Style Black Bean Soup 260

Curried Cauliflower Steaks with Lemon Dressing and Pickled Raisins 264

Butternut Squash Ravioli with Sage Beurre Monté 268

OCEAN 272

Live Day Boat Scallop Crudo with Caviar Chive Vinaigrette 272

Crisp-Skinned Striped Bass with Corn Risotto and Chanterelle Mushrooms 274

Paupiettes of Dover Sole with Shrimp Mousseline, Sea Beans,
and Caviar-Chive Sauce 278

PASTURE 282

Eight-Hour Barbecue Beef Ribs with Chipotle-Orange Spice Rub 282

Duck Breast Pastrami with Roasted Parsnips and Sweet and Sour Shallots 286

SIDES 290

    Roasted Acorn Squash with Apple-Ginger Butter 290

DESSERT 292

    Apple Cider Doughnuts with Caramel Sauce 292

    Pumpkin Cheesecake with Gingersnap Cookie Crust 296

WINTER

GARDEN 302

    Roasted Sweet Potato with Lentils and Roasted Mushrooms. 302

    Chestnut Gnocchi with Butter Sauce and Mixed Winter Vegetables 306

OCEAN 310

    Thai Lobster Bisque En Croûte 310

    Olive Oil Braised Octopus with Hummus and Preserved Lemon Gremolata. 314

    Herb-Crusted Atlantic Cod with Seasonal Mushrooms and Parsley Sauce. 318

    Beaver Kill Trout with Broccoli, Heirloom Carrots,

    Shaved Fingerlings, and Pomegranate-Blood Orange. 322

PASTURE 326

    Seared Venison Chop and Raviolo with Celery Root-Apple Purée. 326

    Milk Braised Ossobuco with Creamy Polenta and Roasted Mushrooms 330

SIDES 334

    Roasted Brussels Sprouts. 334

    Black Winter Truffle Gnocchi. 336

DESSERT 340

    Rum Butterscotch Bread Pudding. 340

    Frosted Root Carrot Cake with Blood Orange Cream Cheese 344

Acknowledgments 346

Metric Conversions. 348

Index 349

PREFACE
BY TOM STRUZZIERI

BUSINESS PARTNER
AND CO-OWNER,
BLACKBARN RESTAURANT

I met John Doherty in grammar school, and we've remained close friends ever since. Even though our careers took separate paths—John pursued food and hospitality while I focused on events, in which I planned, organized, and managed various promotional, business, and social venues—we remained on a parallel path.

Many years later, when we both felt the timing was right, we reconnected and merged our talents to create BLACKBARN Restaurant. We haven't looked back since, as our culinary endeavor continues to reflect nothing but success.

Of course, we find owning and operating a restaurant, especially in New York City, comes with plenty of challenges that require great care. Fortunately, with John at the helm, who, incidentally, has always believed in, and continues to stress the importance of providing the best guest experience we can, the quality of the food we serve doesn't end with what's on the plate. He and I agree it's the warm and engaging hospitality we provide, from the moment a guest walks through our door and feels cared for, until the time they leave, that creates a long-lasting memory.

John and I continue to devote a great many of our resources to delivering that ultimate experience for each and every guest while continuing to exceed their every expectation. That's why I'm so fortunate and honored to have John as my business partner.

When John first approached me with the idea of assembling a BLACKBARN cookbook filled with many of our signature dishes, I was excited from the start. Now, here we are, eager to share with you what we have created along with the keys to our success so others like yourself can experience the same joy as we have. This book further represents yet another step in our exciting journey as we continue to set our sights on a bright and promising future. Enjoy.

MY CULINARY JOURNEY

BY JOHN DOHERTY

Growing up on Long Island, New York, wasn't exactly the epicenter of gastronomy, although I do remember watching my fair share of the *Galloping Gourmet*, which I found entertaining but not inspiring. I also got a taste of some delicious food at my grandmother's table. Grandma was really my step-grandma as my fraternal grandmother had passed away after childbirth. Grandma was of Czechoslovakian descent and deftly skilled at roast duck with sauerkraut, fresh roasted ham with a magnificent gravy, and unforgettable peach dumplings. Ahhh . . . those dumplings, something I looked forward to each year. I also remember watching her put the boiled potatoes through a ricer and adding eggs and flour to make the dough. She would wrap ripe, juicy peaches completely in the dough and boil them in salted water until they floated. Then she'd spoon them onto a platter, split them in half, and drizzle melted butter over the top along with a sprinkling of cinnamon sugar. After Grandma left this Earth, my mother would try her hand at making the peach dumplings, but it was never the same. Outside of the holiday meals at Grandma's, I grew up on home cooked meals void of fast food, soda, and snacks.

Like so many other chefs, I got my start in the kitchen—at the dish machine and pot sink. When there weren't any dirty dishes left, I'd be pulled away to bread shrimp, clean string beans, and wash lettuce. While doing that, I was able to watch the chef and his team of cooks turn my work into something different and enticing, if not magical.

When the opportunity to finally cook presented itself, life as I knew it changed forever. For so many of us, cooking is almost spiritual. It touches our souls like music does for some and art for others. Today, when I'm cooking, people will often say to me "you look so serious." The fact is, I'm focused, connected, and submersed into the food I'm preparing. I'm in a headspace that removes me from all other thoughts and allows me mental and emotional freedom and joy in knowing I am crafting something for someone else's pleasure.

As a cook, developing my skills and deciding to pursue "Chef" status, suddenly more responsibilities entered the picture. Tasks like food purchasing, recipe documentation, employee scheduling, kitchen sanitation standards, developing and implementing standards for employee job performance, fixing plumbing leaks, repairing equipment, and an endless list of other distractions can make cooking with passion and love very difficult. Being highly organized and disciplined is the key to a quiet and focused kitchen. At BLACKBARN, we have an open kitchen with a Chef's Table that sits within five feet of our stove. Guests often ask us why our culinary team isn't talking like those chefs on television,

always hollering and being extremely vocal? Our answer is simple yet difficult to achieve, and that's leadership. An effective leader hires the right people, offers career development with crystal clear instructions, makes sure the proper tools are available to them, and demonstrates the desired results and rewards them when the job is done right. A well-run, classic, professional kitchen is similar to the military in the sense that there is a clear chain of command, uncompromising quality standards, and selfless teamwork amidst challenging conditions. The kitchen is hot, busy, stressful, and physical yet exciting, inspiring, and rewarding. After fifty years as a chef, I can't think of anything else I would rather be.

After cooking at a number of local restaurants on Long Island during my high school years, I attended the Culinary Institute of America (CIA) in Hyde Park, New York. Arguably the premier culinary school in the country, if not the world. The CIA set me up for success. I was hired by the Waldorf Astoria Hotel in New York at nineteen years old—starting as a Tournant (roundsman) working multiple stations in multiple kitchens.

The Waldorf Astoria remains a memorable and iconic institution. Its rich heritage dates back to the late 1800s when it once stood where the Empire State Building stands today. In 1931, the Waldorf moved to Park Avenue and 50th Street. The Waldorf continues to build upon its legacy of hosting the world's most prominent socialites, dignitaries, and premier events. For years, the Waldorf became the training ground for so many successful hoteliers, including myself. If the Waldorf was a school, it would be an Ivy League institution because of its sheer volume, size, and its endless pursuit of excellence. To better understand its size, let me share with you the general layout when I was there. Fourteen hundred guest rooms and suites occupied the building. The entire second floor made up the main kitchen, which was an entire city block. There were two butcher shops, one for meat and fish and the other for poultry, a Garde Manger (cold kitchen), which consisted of a chef, thirteen cooks, a three-person sauce station, a three-person soup kitchen, and a pastry shop which was operated eighteen hours a day by thirteen pastry chefs and cooks. There was also a vegetable cutting room, banquet production room, a twenty-four-hour room service kitchen, and a silver polishing room. Then came the third floor, which housed the Grand Ballroom and five reception rooms that welcomed fifteen hundred guests. The Ballroom kitchen was also on the third floor along with the employee cafeteria, which alone fed more than seven hundred employees a day. Heading up to the fourth floor, one would find several smaller event rooms which held anywhere from twenty

to one hundred and fifty guests and a complete kitchen to service those events. All the way up on the eighteenth floor was the Starlight Roof, which held six hundred guests and its own kitchen to service those guests.

Although I was the youngest appointed Executive Chef in 1985, it took me several years to get there. I was first hired to replace cooks from various kitchens when they went on vacation or took time off. This provided me with a lot of experience in a relatively short time and gave Chef Arno Schmidt a clear idea of my capabilities. Soon thereafter, I was scheduled to the Garde Manger department, which produced all of the cold items for banquets. The pace was furious, from the early hours to five o'clock in the evening. Everyone worked at a frenetic pace with a competitive mentality. If you were the last one to finish a task, you were ridiculed as a "shoemaker." I'm not exactly sure how the term originated or if it was used industry-wide, but you sure didn't want to be called a shoemaker.

Besides the massive catering events, I was also in charge of overseeing three restaurant kitchens—the Peacock Alley fine dining restaurant, the Bull and Bear Steakhouse, and Oscars, which was an all-day dining restaurant. To help me manage these three restaurants were seven highly qualified chefs who helped oversee one hundred fifty cooks and a ninety-person stewarding department.

Moving up the culinary ladder, my next position was manning the sauté station in Peacock Alley. This station was extremely challenging as it not only served the à la carte food for the restaurant, but also for the Marco Polo Club, and room service for the fourteen hundred rooms. This is where I learned how to cook under pressure. Meanwhile, Chef Schmidt would be personally finishing the dishes for those who had permanent residences at the Waldorf like Imelda Marcos, Frank Sinatra, the Ambassador to the United Nations, and many CEOs of major banks.

After one year at the sauté station, Chef Schmidt promoted me to be the assistant to the Chef Saucier in the Main Kitchen. I quickly discovered virtually everyone wanted to work at the sauce station because the station carried a lot of prestige, as the sauces were created for all the events.

When Chef Schmidt resigned from the Waldorf after ten years of service, he was replaced by French Chef Daniel Vigier. Chef Vigier was loud, abrasive, and hellbent on changing everything. Soon, the Chef Saucier left and Chef Vigier appointed me to be the Chef Saucier. It was an amazing challenge in which I thrived. Having to focus all day on making the perfect sauces for both the banquets and all the restaurants now, allowed me to refine my palate and fine cooking skills. One year later, Chef Vigier promoted me to be his Sous Chef. However, I politely declined

WORLD LEADER DINNERS

Every year during the United Nations General Assembly (UNGA), close to twenty-five heads of state from around the world would stay in the Waldorf Towers where security was tight, tensions were high, and the pressure was on. During my twenty-three years as Chef of the Waldorf, I had the privilege and honor to cook for and meet noteworthy world leaders, including many Presidents of the United States. When shaking hands with men like President Ronald Reagan, George Bush, and Bill Clinton, I felt a sense of awe for getting to play a small part in gatherings that were often pivotal in international matters. During the United Nations 40th Anniversary, President Reagan hosted a dinner for the leaders of the free world including Margaret Thatcher, Helmut Kohl, Brian Mulroney, Yasuhiro Nakasone, Benedetto Craxi, and President Francois Mitterand. Before dinner ended, President Reagan, always a gentleman, excused himself from the table to extend his gratitude to me and my team for a successful dinner meeting. Today at BLACKBARN, we offer a "World Leaders Menu" that consists of dishes that were prepared for various leaders during my tenure.

because I still had so much to learn. But Chef Vigier would not take no for an answer. He said he'd teach me everything I needed to know.

At age twenty-four, I was now the Sous Chef at the Waldorf—still one of the largest and most complex hotels in the world. Chef Vigier kept to his word and tutored me on all aspects of becoming a chef. He also shared his thoughts and perceptions, and together we created new dishes and rolled out new menus. Unfortunately, Chef Vigier's continual abrasiveness was too much for the General Manager. He let Vigier go and replaced him with Chef Kurt Earman, who had been the Executive Sous Chef and a father figure to me. Because of our working relationship together, Chef Earman elevated me to the Executive Sous Chef position.

It wasn't long after, while working as the Executive Sous Chef, that an unbelievable opportunity presented itself. A Dutchman named Gerard Fagel, whom I'd met at the Waldorf, offered me the chance to hone my culinary skills in Europe—for free. He set me up in two- and three-star Micheline kitchens in Holland, Belgium, and France. During this time, I discovered the difference between the elite kitchens in Europe and the kitchens at the Waldorf. In Europe, there was a genuine passion and commitment to achieving perfection. I learned one's effort was the difference between good and great. When I returned to the Waldorf, I was filled with passion, ambition, and ideas. I had a vision to bring the Waldorf kitchens to the same level of inspiration that I had experienced in Europe. Two years later, Chef Earman decided to retire and Fred Kleisner, the Managing Director of the Hotel, appointed me to be the new Executive Chef at just twenty-seven years old. I remained the Executive Chef at the Waldorf for twenty-three years while fulfilling my vision of building an inspired and committed team.

To me, building the "dream team," was vitally important. I became obsessed with trying to understand how to get my entire team to work with a shared vision of greatness. One day, I had an epiphany to implement dog training techniques. That's right, dog training. Our family dog, Shannon, was a boxer who loved to play with kids. Unfortunately, Shannon didn't know her own strength, so she'd pounce on children while being playful, knocking them down, and making them cry. That's when we decided to take Shannon to a trainer. What I quickly learned during training is that a dog will connect a command with an action and then a reward, be it a voice inflection, petting, a treat, or all three. In simpler terms, a dog will obey a command to get a reward. I began to implement the same techniques of positive reinforcement with my team. The results were immediate and profound. The more I recognized good work, the more I received. The more I praised a team, the more they worked like a team. The more I asked for input, the more my team started thinking and contributing to the process. In a very short time, my team became inspired to work through problems independently, take ownership of their work, and support each other in the process. Without question, discovering and acquiring proven leadership and business skills have been instrumental in preparing me for what was in store—becoming an independent restaurateur in one of the most competitive markets in the world.

A NEW BEGINNING

Feeling it was time to break out on my own and enjoy the freedom and challenges of entrepreneurship, I got together with a couple of trusted and respected colleagues to take a leap of faith into the restaurant world. Unfortunately, we couldn't raise enough money to open a new restaurant. However, we did land our first consulting gig on Long Island. This led to more consulting jobs, which included restaurant openings, turn-arounds, design, and even developing food for retail. Although I had projects to keep me busy, I never stopped looking for *my* restaurant. Realtors called me weekly, and off I went to look at a space, but nothing ever felt quite right. I started to second guess myself. Was I afraid of failing? Did the Waldorf protect and insulate me too much? One afternoon, I met with my realtor again. This time, he showed me a very large restaurant named SD26, short for San Domenico on 26th street.

SD26 was owned by Tony May and had been open for several years when Tony decided to sell. Tony was a famous and influential restaurateur who I knew personally from my days of sitting on various committees at CIA with many other industry leaders. Tony once owned the Rainbow Room at Rockefeller Center and the highly successful San Domenico restaurant on Central Park South. When the landlord raised the rent, Tony left and built SD26.

I remember the tour with my realtor like it was yesterday—even the very spot where I stood and knew in my bones this would be my restaurant. Immediately, I thought of everything I needed to make my restaurant succeed—and the numbers had to work on paper. I wanted a large restaurant to achieve some economies of scale; an open kitchen to connect with my guests while providing a form of entertainment; an event space which often generates the highest profit margin in a restaurant; and

a sizable bar which has the second highest profit margin. When Tony and I eventually reconnected to talk about the space, I could tell he was happy that his crown jewel would be in the hands of someone he knew.

I now was faced with the daunting task of raising the money to buy and build out the restaurant. After pitching several potential investors, it was my childhood friend, Tom Struzierri, who came through in a big way.

I immediately got to work. I brought in Mark Zeff, a talented architect and interior designer, to get started on several concepts I had in mind for the new restaurant. Having spent thirty years in white-gloved butler service, silver trays, plush drapes, and gilded ceilings at the Waldorf, I wanted the complete opposite aesthetically while the high-quality food, beverage, and service would remain. Mark and I came up with elements that included steel, concrete, wood, and leather—somewhat of a country feel but with an industrial look. While continuing to work on the design, Mark and his wife Kristen invited my wife Jennifer and I out to their home in East Hampton for the weekend. Mark designed the home, which was featured in several architectural magazines. Mark had branded his home design and was rolling it out in the Hamptons at the time. He called his home *Blackbarn*. Immediately I thought to myself, what an amazing name for my restaurant. Days later, when Mark and I entered the dining room of the restaurant to visualize our design concepts, I asked Mark what he would think if I called it Blackbarn, expecting a left hook to my jaw. Mark turned to me and said, "Absolutely! I love it!" Then he scribbled something on a piece of paper, handed it to me, and said, "Here's your barn!" He'd drawn the rafters that are now a signature of BLACKBARN restaurant. Sheer brilliance. Mark went on to design the rest of the building without any details overlooked. He viewed the building as if it was a blank canvas, transforming a contemporary space into a modern barn with rustic finishes, refined lines, and industrial touches. I, meanwhile, focused on the China, glassware, staff uniforms, music, and menu. At BLACKBARN, my goal has always been to create a space where guests feel at home— comfortable, relaxed, and free to be themselves—while enjoying elevated food and wine without the pretentiousness of fine dining.

My new business partner, Tom, had his contractor, Joe Wilson, come down from Saugerties, NY to help Mark's team to renovate and transform the restaurant in just seven weeks. We opened to the public in September of 2015, and I've never looked back.

BLACKBARN has been a blessing to me in so many ways. Not a day goes by that I don't stop somewhere in the restaurant and feel a sense of gratitude. People often ask me which life I prefer, being the Chef of

the Waldorf or the owner of BLACKBARN? The answer is easy—I'll take entrepreneurship any day. Of course, owning a business comes with its own set of challenges, as there's a lot more at stake owning a restaurant. But for me, the real joy comes in many forms—the freedom to make choices and the ability to change on a dime; exercising creativity; watching guests laugh and enjoy themselves; the appreciation for the team who comes together to create magic day in and day out and do it with a smile; and knowing my efforts are providing a comfortable life for my family. I am living the reality of a dream that I held in my heart and in my mind, and prayed would happen one day. Today is living proof of that.

Today, what gives me the greatest motivation and fulfillment to keep going is the joy in serving others. Sharing with our guests what my team and I have created and what we get excited about, be it a new dessert, our latest appetizer, wine or whiskey, is what makes it all worthwhile. I find cooking for others an act of love. Love is a form of energy, and I can feel that energy while I'm cooking. Writing this cookbook is a wonderful way to share our story. We are happy to serve others, we love to see people enjoy themselves, we are proud of what we have accomplished, and we're happy to share our recipes and stories that bring us so much joy at BLACKBARN with you.

GIVING BACK

I had mentioned earlier that I used to offer consulting services. One of those services was working with the Chicken Soup for the Soul brand, who had asked me to develop a full line of retail food products, starting with chicken soup. Near the end of that project, I remember perusing the grocery store where I came across Uncle Ben's "Ready Cook Rice" in a pouch. Then I saw tuna in a pouch and wondered, *how can this be possible? If I tried putting food in a pouch at room temperature it would certainly blow up like a balloon and be thrown out,* so I spoke to my food scientist friend, John Randazzi at Eatem Foods in New Jersey where I developed most of the recipes for Chicken Soup for the Soul. John explained, "the pouch is the 'new can.'" The materials can withstand high temperatures to sterilize the ingredients and give them an eighteen-to-twenty-four-month shelf life. I asked John if the tuna could go in with rice. He answered yes. What about vegetables and sauce? I then asked. He smiled and said that I could add anything I wanted, as long as each ingredient hits that temperature of sterilization. As I drove home on the New Jersey Turnpike after our meeting, I felt a calling to make complete meals in a pouch and distribute them to those in need. As the tears rolled down my face, I immediately saw the name—Heavenly HARVST—and its logo in my mind. In the days that followed, I filed for a 501(c)(3), forming my not-for-profit organization. Before I knew it, in 2014, the organization was formed. Today, we have made and distributed more than 300,000 meals to people and communities in need around the country. The team, up until recently, was made up of my daughter, Jenna Elliot, and myself. Several months ago, I began expanding the board and scaling the organization to reach more people. Today, it consists of industry leaders who share a common interest in helping to eliminate food insecurity. You can learn more about what we do and how we do it at HeavenlyHARVST.org.

GOING GREEN

Without much intention, BLACKBARN became a "green" restaurant from day one. This was thanks, in part, to our mission of sourcing as much local produce, cheese, meat, and fish as possible while producing as little waste as we could. What started out as a means to save money, landed us in a place that many companies and individuals are drawn to because of our philosophical alignment. Additionally, our efforts to conserve energy and resources have gone far beyond our expectations and much to our benefit too. BLACKBARN is a very large restaurant and with that comes a hefty utility bill, which was aggravating me every month when I saw the bill. My first opportunity to reduce that bill was to convert all our light bulbs and dimmers to LEDs, saving us thousands of dollars. Soon, all five of our air-conditioning units were placed on a computerized schedule to work only during service. These cost saving initiatives created a shift in our thinking while helping us to find greener alternatives to many of our former practices. We stopped buying water bottles and started using empty wine and liquor bottles for our water service. We also make small serving boards for our doughnuts and hors d'oeuvres from our wooden wine boxes. We made the change from plastic to recyclable take-out plates and flatware. When New York City began a composting program, we signed on and started working with a composting company originally named Peat which now goes by AfterLife. AfterLife takes our food scraps, turns them into compost, then grows a variety of mushrooms which we then buy at a discount and use in recipes like our Mushroom Toast (page 164). Simultaneously, there was an initiative started in our neighborhood of NoMad to get as many restaurants as possible to become Certified Green by the Green Restaurant Association. Once we were inspected, we received our certification based on all the points we had accumulated. Much to our surprise, we now have companies and individuals reaching out to make event and dining reservations based on our green initiative alone. Truly a winning endeavor we are proud of and will continue to support.

MORE ABOUT TOM STRUZZIERI— FRIENDS FIRST, BUSINESS PARTNERS SECOND

Tom and I go back to our days at St. Philip Niery, a Catholic school, from grades 1–8 in East Northport, Long Island. Tom had been attending their grammar school, and I enrolled in the seventh grade. We met in a fistfight on the school playground. To this day, I don't know how or why it began, but it was over almost as soon as it started. What I do remember clearly was a male teacher taking us by the ear to the principal's office. As we waited outside the office of Sister Paul Frances, Tom (who was a school gem) said to me, "We'd better make up now before she gets here." So we shook hands, and as soon as the door opened, Tom said, "Sister, we made up, and we're friends now." She smiled and told us to go on our way. Tom was the big man on campus, even at fourteen! We quickly became best of friends, spending days waterskiing off his boat, camping out on the beach, and picking up chicks along the way. At least, that was always the mission—but with little to no success, we had fun talking about it. As we entered high school, we played football together—Tom was the fullback, and I was the left tackle. His headstrong determination served him well as he plowed up the middle. To this day, Tom loves talking about our time in Home Economics class, where he insists he outperformed me behind the range, which is entirely possible, but in the end, I can make a better omelet. Tom wound up as school president with high honors while I found my calling to become a chef. At graduation, when our classmates voted Best This and Best That, Tom and I were both voted Student Most Likely to Succeed.

After graduation, I went off to attend the Culinary Institute of America in Hyde Park, New York, and Tom attended Vassar College just a few miles away. In our second year, Tom and his dad bought a horse stable called Roseview Stables, where Tom was the owner/operator, and I took a room in his house while attending chef school. Time passed, and we were each the best man at each other's weddings. Although family, distance, and ambition allowed us to drift a bit, we stayed in touch. Tom became extremely successful in the equestrian business as the owner of HITS (Horse Shows in the Sun), which has show grounds in Saugerties, New York; Virginia; Ocala, Florida; California, Chicago; and Vermont. We came back together in a big way when Tom created and built the Diamond Mills Hotel in Saugerties in 2010. I had just left the Waldorf and was able to help design the kitchens and develop the food and beverage operation while I looked for a restaurant for myself in New York City.

Over the years, I had pursued having my own restaurant and had difficulty raising the capital to do it. Even Tom had no appetite for investing in a New York City high-risk restaurant venture, so when I found the BLACKBARN location on 26th Street in Manhattan, I went to Tom for advice on how to raise the capital. I needed a sizable down payment and would need an even larger sum a few months later, so I asked Tom if he knew anyone interested in backing me. Tom asked to look over what I thought was a pretty compelling business plan, so I sent it for him to review. About a week later, he suggested I come and discuss the plan. Based on previous conversations, I really thought Tom had some questions or advice. I hoped that he knew someone who could get me started. My wife Jennifer and I took the ride to visit Tom and sat in his office; after chatting and catching up on life, we turned our attention to the business plan. I explained again how I was looking for a down payment loan that a more significant sum would follow.

Tom had several questions, which we reviewed, and then, with a slight pause, he slid the business plan across the desk to me and said, "I'm not interested in the down payment, but I will fund the entire project." Well, I was in shock a bit. I remember my head spinning in disbelief—so many thoughts and emotions going on. Excitement, relief, joy, gratitude, and fear all mixed together. It took a few days to sink in that my dream just might come true. Eventually, we closed on the restaurant, and after the closing, Tom came to look at the restaurant for the first time. His comment to me was, "This is a better deal than I thought." That made me happy to know that I didn't mislead my friend and that my new partner was even more comfortable than when he decided to invest. Like every business, there are highs and lows, but as time goes on, we both know that we are friends first and partners second. Now, that's an easy thing to say, but it plays into the decisions we make. Tom supports most decisions I make in running the business, but when he doesn't agree with me on something, he sometimes gives in, partly because he trusts me and partly because he puts our friendship first, and letting an unnecessary argument come between us is not worth it.

On the other hand, I make every business decision with Tom in mind, protecting his investment and trust in me. I will forgo something that's important to me to preserve our friendship because that is more valuable to me than anything in business. The magic for me is not just that I have a continued reason to keep and build a friendship but that my best friend gave me the opportunity of a lifetime and allowed my dream to become a reality. It's such a great story, and this book has given me the opportunity to tell it to the world.

INGREDIENTS AND PANTRY

Below, you'll find information about some of the less common, possibly unfamiliar ingredients in this book: what they taste like, where to find them, and notes—where relevant—about their fascinating role at BLACKBARN. This isn't meant to be an exhaustive list, but rather a quick primer on foods in our recipes that are specific to our style of cuisine.

MEAT AND SEAFOOD

AMISH CHICKEN
Amish chicken refers to poultry raised following traditional, sustainable farming practices associated with the Amish community. These chickens are typically raised in small, family-run farms where they have access to free-range environments, allowing them to forage naturally. This method results in meat that is often leaner and more flavorful compared to conventionally raised chicken. Amish farmers prioritize animal welfare, avoiding the use of antibiotics and growth hormones, and focus on providing a natural diet and living conditions. The meat from Amish chickens is known for its rich taste and texture, which we find superior, especially when making our Grilled Amish Chicken with Chimichurri and Panzanella Salad (page 236).

ATLANTIC DAY BOAT SCALLOPS
Atlantic Day Boat scallops are a premium type of sea scallop, prized for their freshness, flavor, and sustainable harvesting methods, as you'll find when we're making our Live Day Boat Scallop Crudo with Caviar Chive Vinaigrette (page 272) or Pan-Seared Day Boat Scallops with Crispy Pancetta and English Pea Risotto (page 188). These scallops are caught by small, independent fishing vessels that venture out to sea and return with their catch within twenty-four hours, ensuring the scallops are exceptionally fresh when they reach the market.

BIGEYE TUNA
Bigeye tuna is a large, fast-swimming tuna found in warm ocean waters.

It is a significant species in both commercial and recreational fishing, often sought after for sushi and sashimi due to its deep red flesh and high fat content, particularly in the belly area, known as "toro." Bigeyes are known for their ability to dive deeper than many other tuna species, reaching depths of over 1,000 meters. They have large eyes, adapted to low-light environments, which give them an advantage in hunting prey in the deep ocean. We prefer Bigeye tuna for its rich flavor and tender texture.

BRANZINO

Branzino, also known as European sea bass, is a prized fish found in the Mediterranean Sea and along the eastern Atlantic coast. Renowned for its delicate, mild flavor and tender, flaky white flesh that's low-fat and clean tasting, branzino is a popular choice at BLACKBARN. Its skin is often silver, with a streamlined body that makes it appealing for grilling, roasting, or baking. We like to serve it whole, as you'll find with our Roasted Branzino with Spiced Roasted Carrots and Pan Roasted Potatoes (page 226), which helps retain moisture and flavor during cooking.

EAST COAST STRIPED BASS

East Coast striped bass, also known as a striper, is a prized species native to the Atlantic coast of North America, ranging from the Gulf of St. Lawrence to Florida. Recognizable by their distinctive horizontal black stripes running along their silver bodies, these fish are highly valued both commercially and recreationally. Striped bass are known for their firm, white flesh and mild, slightly sweet flavor, making them a popular choice for us, especially when making our Crisp-Skinned Striped Bass with Corn Risotto and Chanterelle Mushrooms (page 274).

HERITAGE "CHESHIRE" PORK

Cheshire pork, named after Cheshire in England, is renowned for its distinctive quality and flavor—perfect for our IPA Braised Cheshire Pork Shank with Charred Tomatillo Relish (page 198). This breed of pig, one of the oldest in Britain, is celebrated for its tender, succulent meat with a rich, well-marbled texture. Cheshire pigs are traditionally reared in a pasture-based system, allowing them to roam and forage, which contributes to the depth of flavor in their pork. The breed has a reputation for producing excellent quality sausages and bacon due to its high fat content and flavorful profile. Cheshire pork has been a staple in British cuisine for centuries, cherished for its traditional and wholesome qualities. Its historical significance and the commitment to preserving traditional farming methods make Cheshire pork a symbol of quality and heritage in British agriculture.

PADDLEFISH CAVIAR

Paddlefish caviar, often referred to as American caviar, comes from the paddlefish, a freshwater species found in US rivers, particularly in Montana and Missouri. Its eggs are similar to those of sturgeon caviar, with a smooth, earthy flavor and a subtle, buttery finish. The pearls are typically small, grayish to black in color, and prized for their delicate texture. Paddlefish caviar is a sustainable alternative to traditional sturgeon varieties, making it a popular choice for many fine dining experiences, especially when we're serving our Live Day Boat Scallop Crudo with Caviar Chive Vinaigrette (page 272) and Paupiettes of Dover Sole with Shrimp Mousseline, Sea Beans, and Caviar-Chive Sauce (page 278).

FRUIT, VEGETABLE, AND OTHER

BELUGA LENTILS

Beluga lentils are small, black lentils named for their resemblance to beluga caviar. Rich in protein, fiber, and nutrients like iron and folate, they have a mild, earthy flavor with a firm texture that holds up well in cooking. These lentils are popular in our salads, soups, or in dishes like our Roasted Sweet Potatoes with Lentils and Roasted Mushrooms (page 302). Unlike other lentils, they don't require soaking and cook quickly, making them a convenient and nutritious addition to various meals.

BLACK MISSION FIGS

Black Mission figs are a sweet, dark-skinned variety of fig, prized for their rich, jammy flavor and soft, chewy texture. Originally from Spain, they have been cultivated in California since the eighteenth century, and we now get ours locally. Their purple-black exterior contrasts with a vibrant pink, seedy interior, making them visually appealing in dishes, such as our Black Mission Fig Pizza (page 256). Black Mission figs can be enjoyed fresh, dried, or cooked in both savory and sweet recipes, offering a high fiber content and essential vitamins like potassium and calcium.

BLACK WINTER TRUFFLES

Black winter truffles (*Tuber melanosporum*), also known as Périgord truffles, are prized edible fungi renowned for their earthy, musky aroma and complex

flavor. Found primarily in Southern Europe, they grow underground, forming symbiotic relationships with tree roots, particularly oak and hazelnut. Harvested in the winter months, these rare truffles are typically foraged using trained dogs or pigs. Their intense, rich taste enhances dishes like our Black Winter Truffle Gnocchi (page 336), as well as other pastas, risottos, and sauces, making them a gourmet delicacy at BLACKBARN.

BLOODY BUTCHER CORNMEAL

Bloody Butcher cornmeal is made from an heirloom variety of corn known for its striking deep red kernels. First cultivated in the 1800s, this corn is highly valued for its rich, nutty flavor and rustic texture. The meal produced from Bloody Butcher corn retains a distinctive red and yellow color, making it as visually unique as its taste. Popular in Southern cooking, it's often used in our traditional dishes like our Blue Corn "Johnny Cakes" (page 114) for added depth and character.

CATSKILL PROVISIONS HONEY

Catskill Provisions honey is a unique, artisanal product sourced from the pristine Catskill Mountains. The region's rich biodiversity and untouched environment result in honey with distinct flavors, reflecting the variety of wildflowers and plants that bees pollinate. This honey is produced using sustainable, small-scale beekeeping methods, ensuring high quality and environmental responsibility. Catskill Provisions honey is prized for its pure, raw form, free from additives, making it a favorite among health-conscious folks like me and many of our BLACKBARN guests. Try it when making our Almond Honey Croissants (page 96).

HUDSON VALLEY PRODUCE

Hudson Valley fresh produce, such as their apples and pears, is celebrated for its exceptional quality, grown in the fertile soil of New York's Hudson Valley. Local farms in the region focus on sustainable, organic practices, offering a wide variety of seasonal fruits and vegetables. The produce is harvested at peak ripeness, ensuring maximum flavor, like what you'll find in our Orange Cardamom Cinnamon Buns (page 102). Hudson Valley's proximity to our two BLACKBARN locations allows for short farm-to-table distances, providing our guests with fresh, vibrant produce that supports local farmers and communities.

LABNEH

Labneh is a rich, creamy Middle Eastern dairy product made by straining yogurt to remove excess whey, resulting in a thick, tangy spread. Often enjoyed as a dip or used as a substitute for cream cheese, labneh has a smooth texture and mildly tart flavor. High in protein and probiotics, labneh is a nutritious addition to such dishes as our Roasted Sweet Potatoes with Lentils and Roasted Mushrooms (page 302) and our Green Goddess Dressing that we toss with our Charred Gem Lettuce (page 112).

MOSCATEL VINEGAR

Moscatel vinegar is a gourmet vinegar made from Moscatel grapes, known for their natural sweetness and floral aroma. Originating in Mediterranean regions, it has a rich, amber color and a balanced flavor profile, combining sweet, tangy, and fruity notes. This vinegar is often used to enhance our salads, dressings, and marinades, adding depth to our dishes. Its distinctive sweetness makes it a versatile ingredient, perfect for our Caviar Chive Vinaigrette used in our Live Day Boat Scallop Crudo (page 272), our Tomato Vinaigrette used in our Grilled Amish Chicken (page 236), and our Sweet and Sour Shallots from our Duck Breast Pastrami recipe (page 286).

SEA BEANS

Sea beans, also known as salicornia or samphire, are succulent plants that grow in coastal marshes and saline environments. They have a crisp texture and a naturally salty flavor, often described as a blend of asparagus and seaweed. Rich in minerals and vitamins, sea beans are popular in gourmet cuisine and frequently used in our salads, garnishes, or sautéed as a side dish. Their unique taste and crunchy texture make them a prized ingredient in our seafood dishes like our Paupiettes of Dover Sole (page 278).

SHISHITO PEPPERS

Shishito peppers are small, mild, and flavorful chili peppers originating from Japan. Typically green and about two to four inches long, these peppers are known for their thin skin and delicate taste. They are often enjoyed in Japanese cuisine, particularly grilled or sautéed. The peppers have a sweet, slightly smoky flavor with a mild heat, although occasionally, one in every ten peppers can be unexpectedly spicy. Shishito peppers are versatile and can be prepared in various ways, such as our blistered Shishito Peppers (page 202).

SPANISH ONIONS

Spanish onions are large, yellow-skinned onions known for their mild, sweet flavor compared to other varieties. They have a high-water content, making them perfect for raw use in our salads, sandwiches, or in our Homemade Fish Stock, which you'll find in our recipe for Paupiettes of Dover Sole with Shrimp Mousseline, Sea Beans, and Caviar-Chive Sauce (page 278). When cooked, the Spanish onions turn tender and add a subtle sweetness to our dishes. Commonly used in Mediterranean and Spanish cuisine, we find them ideal for caramelizing or sautéing, and their size makes them convenient for our recipes requiring a large onion yield.

ZA'ATAR SPICE

Za'atar is a popular Middle Eastern spice blend made from dried thyme, oregano, sumac, sesame seeds, and sometimes other herbs. It has a savory, tangy flavor, with the sumac adding a citrusy note. We'll sprinkle this spice over flatbreads, mixed with olive oil for a dip, or used as a seasoning for our roasted meats and vegetables, like our Roasted Heirloom Carrots with English Pea Hummus (page 180) and Roasted Sweet Potatoes (page 302). We find Za'atar's bold flavor elevates our dishes with a distinctive herbal and nutty taste.

HOW TO USE THIS BOOK TO EAT AND DRINK THROUGH THE SEASONS

Using a seasonal cookbook like ours is a transformative approach to cooking that embraces the natural rhythm of the seasons. Not only does this book represent our favorite dishes that we enjoy making and serving at BLACKBARN, but it also offers you—the home cook—an opportunity to cook and serve the same delicious meals and drinks at home by harnessing the freshest, most flavorful ingredients at their peak. This culinary philosophy not only brings variety and nutrition to the table but creates a deeper connection to nature, local agriculture, and sustainable food practices.

THE CONCEPT OF SEASONAL COOKING

At the heart of our book is the idea that nature provides exactly what we need at different times of the year. The ingredients available in each season reflect the weather, environment, and nutritional needs. For example, in the summer, we find an abundance of juicy fruits like berries and peaches, which help hydrate and cool us down, while the colder months provide hearty root vegetables and citrus fruits packed with vitamin C, ideal for warming meals and supporting the immune system.

As you'll discover in the pages ahead, we designed our book to guide you in aligning your cooking with what nature offers. We also feature our recipes that are crafted around ingredients harvested in the spring, summer, autumn, and winter, ensuring that the dishes you make highlight the freshest flavors of the season.

BENEFITS OF USING A SEASONAL COOKBOOK

MAXIMIZING FLAVOR

Seasonal ingredients are at their peak in terms of flavor and nutrition. When fruits, vegetables, and herbs are harvested at the right time, they are richer in taste and more vibrant in color. For example, tomatoes picked in the height of summer are sweet, juicy, and full of flavor, making them perfect for salads, sauces, or fresh salsas. Our book will guide you to recipes that allow you to highlight these peak ingredients, ensuring that every dish is packed with flavor.

SUPPORTING LOCAL AND SUSTAINABLE AGRICULTURE

By using our cookbook, you are encouraged to seek out local produce, as seasonal cooking often aligns with what is grown and harvested by nearby farms. Buying locally reduces the environmental impact of long-distance transportation and supports small-scale, sustainable agriculture. This, in turn, strengthens the local economy and ensures you are consuming food that is grown with care for the environment.

Local farmers' markets become a treasure trove of inspiration, offering freshly picked produce that you can immediately incorporate into your meals. Our book will help guide you toward the best ingredients and even introduce you to some new ingredients you may not find in a typical grocery store.

NUTRITIONAL BENEFITS

Eating seasonally isn't just about taste—it's about nutrition. Fruits and vegetables lose nutrients over time, especially when they are stored for long periods or transported over long distances. Seasonal cooking encourages the consumption of produce that has been harvested recently, providing you with ingredients that are nutrient-dense and packed with vitamins, minerals, and antioxidants. For example, during autumn, you might cook with winter squash and sweet potatoes, which are rich in beta-carotene, while spring brings fresh greens like spinach and asparagus, loaded with iron and folate.

SEASONAL COOKING THROUGH THE YEAR

SPRING

Spring is a time of renewal, and the produce reflects this with fresh, green, and delicate flavors. Our spring chapter will focus on light and bright dishes that highlight the first harvests of the year. Expect recipes featuring white asparagus, peas, carrots, and shishito peppers, along with fresh crab, clams, scallops, lamb, and pork, as well as our Chocolate Soufflé (page 206) and Roasted Figs and Almond Shortbread with Whipped Ricotta (page 210).

SUMMER

Summer is abundant with vibrant, juicy, and flavorful produce. Tomatoes, zucchini, corn, kale, and watermelon are in full swing, making it a great time for grilling and creating fresh salads and sides. Our book will guide you to recipes that make the most of these ingredients, along with fresh seafood like shrimp, lobster, tuna, and branzino as well as succulent chicken and steaks, perfect for the grill.

Fruit is also at its peak in the summer, and our book will include a variety of recipes for using berries, peaches, and more. Desserts like our Pavlova with Summer Fruit (page 248) and Summer Berry Zabaglione with Lemon Lady Fingers (page 252) will bring the taste of summer to your table.

AUTUMN

As the weather cools, our appetites turn toward heartier, warmer dishes. Fall is the season for pumpkins, squash, cauliflower, and apples and root vegetables like parsnips and shallots. Our autumn chapter will include recipes that showcase these comforting ingredients, such as our Butternut Squash Ravioli (page 268), Crisp-Skinned Striped Bass (page 274), Duck Breast Pastrami (page 286), and Roasted Acorn Squash (page 290) and Roasted Parsnips (page 286).

Autumn also brings an array of spices like cinnamon, nutmeg, and cloves, which pair perfectly with our Apple Cider Doughnuts with Caramel Sauce (page 292) and our creamy Pumpkin Cheesecake (page 296).

WINTER

Winter cooking is all about warmth, comfort, and nourishment. Brussels sprouts, sweet potatoes, mushrooms, and truffles are the stars of the season. Our winter chapter will offer recipes that create warmth from the inside out, such as our Chestnut Gnocchi (page 306), Herb-Crusted Atlantic Cod (page 318), Seared Venison Chop (page 326), and Rum Butterscotch Bread Pudding (page 340).

We now invite you to explore the exciting pages and seasonal recipes ahead while encouraging you to make our favorite dishes that are flavorful, fresh, and hopefully deepen your connection to the natural world and local communities. By cooking with ingredients that are in season, you can celebrate the changing of the seasons and create dishes that reflect the time of year. From the first bright flavors of spring to the comforting warmth of winter meals, our book will guide you through the year, helping you serve delicious meals and drinks that are as diverse as the seasons themselves.

TOOLS AND EQUIPMENT

As important as having the necessary ingredients on hand, having the right kitchen tools is an essential part of cooking efficiently and successfully. From basic barware and blenders to the right pans and appliances, the following tools play a vital role in our cooking process both at my home and at BLACKBARN. Investing in quality utensils also ensures smoother preparation and better-tasting dishes. Here's a short list of some kitchen tools I like to keep at the ready.

BLENDER

A kitchen blender is a versatile appliance used to mix, purée, or emulsify food and liquids. It's perfect for making our smoothies, soups, sauces, and more. With sharp blades powered by a motor, it quickly processes ingredients, saving time and effort in meal preparation. Durable and essential in modern kitchens.

FOOD PROCESSOR

A food processor is a versatile kitchen appliance designed to chop, slice, shred, and purée ingredients quickly. With various blade attachments, it can handle tasks like making dough, grating cheese, or chopping vegetables. Its powerful motor and large capacity make it ideal for saving time during meal prep.

STAND MIXER

A stand mixer is a powerful kitchen tool designed for hands-free mixing, kneading, and whipping. With a motorized base and various attachments, it effortlessly handles our dough, batter, and other ingredients. Ideal for baking, it ensures consistent results, making it an essential appliance for home cooks and professionals alike.

FINE MESH STRAINERS

Fine mesh kitchen strainers are versatile tools used to sift, strain, and drain ingredients. Their tightly woven mesh catches small particles, making them ideal for rinsing our grains, sifting flour, or straining sauces.

Durable and easy to clean, they're essential for achieving smooth, lump-free results in cooking and baking.

KITCHEN SPIDER
A kitchen spider is a handy tool with a wide, flat, wire-mesh basket and a long handle. It's perfect for lifting and draining our fried foods, noodles, or vegetables from hot oil or boiling water. Its design allows for quick, efficient draining while keeping our hands safely away from heat.

MORTAR AND PESTLE
A mortar and pestle are traditional kitchen tools used for grinding and crushing ingredients like herbs, spices, and garlic. Made from stone, wood, or ceramic, it allows for manual control over texture, creating finely ground or coarsely crushed results. It's essential for authentic flavor in many of our dishes.

RING MOLDS, COOKIE CUTTERS, AND TART RINGS
Ring molds are versatile kitchen tools used in our baking and food presentation. Typically made of metal or silicone, they come in various sizes and shapes, from classic round to intricate designs. Ring molds are perfect for assembling beautifully shaped dishes, such as Bigeye Tuna Tartare (page 220), allowing you to showcase your creativity and precision.

KITCHEN THERMOMETER
A kitchen thermometer is an essential tool for precise cooking, ensuring meats, poultry, and baked goods reach the perfect internal temperature. It also helps prevent undercooking or overcooking, promoting food safety and quality. Whether digital or analog, we find thermometers invaluable for achieving professional-level results in home and professional kitchens.

ICE CREAM MAKER
An ice cream maker allows us to create delicious, customized frozen treats with ease. From classic vanilla to creative flavors, both home and commercial ice cream makers offer endless possibilities. With control over ingredients, it's perfect for those seeking healthier, homemade options. Enjoy fresh, creamy ice cream anytime, right from your kitchen.

CAST IRON SKILLETS

Cast iron skillets are a versatile kitchen staple for us. Best known for their durability and excellent heat retention, they're perfect for frying, baking, and searing while the skillet develops a natural non-stick surface over time. Suitable for stovetop or oven use, these skillets can last generations, making them a favorite among home cooks and professional chefs alike.

WAFFLE IRON

A waffle iron is a handy kitchen appliance designed to create crispy, golden waffles. With its heated plates forming the iconic grid pattern, it ensures even cooking and perfect texture. Whether for breakfast or dessert, waffle irons make it easy to enjoy homemade waffles with our favorite toppings.

OUTDOOR GRILL

If your home allows for an outdoor grill, it offers the perfect way to grill meats, vegetables, and more. Whether gas, charcoal, or electric, a good-quality grill brings a smoky flavor and a social experience to cooking, whether at home or at the restaurant. Durable and versatile, the outdoor grill will also transform your backyard into a culinary hotspot.

COOKING TECHNIQUES

DRY HEAT COOKING

Dry heat cooking methods use heat without moisture to cook food, resulting in rich tastes and crispy textures. Examples include grilling, roasting, and sautéing. These methods are ideal for meats, vegetables, and breads, helping to develop complex flavors through caramelization and Maillard reactions.

BROILING

This is when food is cooked from an overhead flame, which will make a nice crispy top; however, the food stands to lose its water or juices from the bottom. This method is more acceptable for thin fish than it is for thicker meats. For thicker meats, if you don't have a grill, rather than broil, brown in a skillet and finish in an oven.

GRILLING

A dry heat method using direct heat. Best grilling temperature ranges from 400°F to 450°F. Make sure the grill is preheated. Oil the grill rack lightly to prevent sticking. Coat the item to be grilled in oil and then season. Thicker cuts are started on the hotter part of the grill and then moved to lower heat. Test for doneness.

BEEF GRILLING TIPS:

Always maintain a clean grill by using a wire brush and wipe with an oiled towel to prevent sticking.

For best results, leave the meat alone. Don't keep turning it. Allow the protein to get a good char before turning and use a digital thermometer to check for doneness. Cutting into a steak or burger prematurely forces the juices to run out, leaving the meat dry.

Never press or smash the burgers down with your spatula. The meat isn't cooking any faster by flattening them, resulting in a dry final product.

Always use a thermometer to determine doneness; never cut into the meat.

Rare (125°F)	Remove at 120°F
Medium Rare (135°F)	Remove at 130°F
Medium (145°F)	Remove at 140°F
Medium Well (150°F)	Remove at 145°F
Well (155°F)	Remove at 150°F

For ground meat: (160°F) as recommended by USDA

Please keep in mind that at whatever temperature you remove the meat, it will continue to cook for another 5 degrees. If you prefer medium rare like I do, remove the meat when the internal temperature reads 130°F.

ROASTING/ BAKING

Roasting is used for more tender cuts such as loins, racks, top and bottom rounds, poultry, and vegetables. As simple as roasting may seem, if it is not done properly, the results can be disastrous. Roasting is done at temperatures anywhere from 250°F to 425°F depending on the item, its size, and the desired results.

ROASTING TIPS:

When roasting meat, for best results, "searing" the meat prior to roasting will create better flavor through caramelization and greater tenderness from a lower roasting temperature.

Searing—Heat a large enough skillet to hold the meat over medium to high heat on the stove with a small amount of oil. Caramelize the meat by browning the meat on all sides, which will seal in the juices during the roasting period and enhance flavor development.

Understand that meat is a muscle that will contract when heat is applied. The higher the heat, the tighter the muscle and faster juices will bleed out and greater shrinkage takes place. Generally, higher temperatures are for smaller cuts that need just a short time in the oven and lower temperatures for larger cuts that need longer cook times.

Checking for doneness—Using a meat thermometer is the most accurate and recommended method for checking doneness in any size cut of meat. We know how quickly a burger or steak can over-cook, so using a thermometer is the best way to ensure proper doneness.

"By feel" is the least accurate method but can work if done by a very experienced cook. If I'm in a pinch, I will insert a metal skewer into the center of the cut and then tap it on the inside of my wrist or the inside of my bottom lip to test for temperature.

Carry-over cooking—Meat does not stop cooking after it is removed from the oven or off the grill. The degree of carry-over cooking will depend on the size of the meat, temperature of the oven, and the temperature of the meat. Therefore, it is necessary to remove the meat from the oven or the grill before it has reached its doneness.

See grill temperatures on the previous page for desired doneness.

Resting the roast is necessary to relax the meat fibers and allow the juice to return to the center of the meat. If resting is not allowed, the meat will bleed extensively when sliced and be very dry. Small steaks should rest for 5–8 minutes while larger roasts need 10–15 minutes.

For larger roasts, jus or pan gravy is obtained by adding a mirepoix (a mix of carrots, onions, and celery) for the last hour of cooking and deglazing the pan with water or stock; thickening is optional. For smaller cuts, deglaze the pan with water, wine or stock to capture the essence of the dish. Be sure to scrape the bottom of the pan to dissolve. The remaining juice and/or solids in the bottom of the roasting pan is called fond, and it's pure gold!

By "deglazing," or dissolving the fond in water, wine, juice, vinegar or sauce, you can increase the intensity and complexity of the flavor for that dish.

SAUTÉING

Many recipes call for sautéing, which is a quick process using a hot pan with a small amount of oil. The term comes from the French word *sauter* which means to jump. The point is the food is best if cooked quickly over high heat to lightly brown the food and retain as much moisture as possible. If the pan being used is too small or overloaded, it will cool down immediately and the food will begin to purge its water, rendering it dry and never allowing caramelization.

SAUTÉING TIPS:

Choose the Proper Cooking Medium: This can be whole butter; clarified butter; oil: olive, avocado, vegetable, etc.; bacon, chicken, or duck fat; or any combination of these.

Choose the proper size pan. Too large of a pan will cause the pan to burn in spots and not allow for deglazing. Too small of a pan will create an overload and reduce the temperature of the pan quickly, therefore not searing properly.

Bring your cooking medium to the perfect temperature-. Oil: just as it begins to ripple; butter, just when the butter stops making a crackling sound.

Blot the product with a paper towel to remove any excess

moisture. This will prevent unnecessary splattering and promote better caramelization.

Add the seasoned product to the pan and brown evenly on both sides. Do not turn product over until it is evenly browned. If the product is browned to the desired point but not fully cooked, finish cooking it in a moderate oven (350°F).

REDUCTION

A frequently used term in recipes. Basically, it refers to evaporating the water and creating a more concentrated liquid. Simmering is the best way to reduce a liquid. Sometimes, that reduced liquid is too salty on its own so replacing the evaporated water with butter will reduce the saltiness and add a richer mouthfeel.

If making a pan gravy for say a turkey or larger roast and a generous amount of gravy is desired, add chicken or beef broth to the pan drippings and reduce to the desired taste. If thickening is desired, a roux (cooked 50/50 flour/butter), Beurre Manie (uncooked 50/50 butter/flour), or a corn starch slurry can be used.

Always check the seasoning throughout and adjust when necessary. Strain through a chinois (fine mesh strainer).

MOIST HEAT COOKING

Unlike dry heat cooking, moist heat cooking involves using liquid or steam to transfer heat, resulting in tender, flavorful dishes. These methods include boiling, braising, poaching, simmering, steaming, and stewing. For irresistibly tender and juicy dishes, explore these cooking techniques:

BOILING

Boiling is best for preparations where rapid cooking is desired, i.e., vegetables, pasta, and reducing liquids or stovetop steaming.

BOILING TIPS:

Water boils at 212°F.

A covered pot will boil much faster than an uncovered pot.

Cooking in salted water allows the salt to penetrate the food and you'll need less at the end. This also prevents your finished product from tasting well-seasoned on the outside, but bland when bitten through.

BRAISING

The braising method of cooking is used for meats with tougher muscle like shoulder and shanks, and there is a need to break down the muscle fibers in order to make it tender. Tenderness is created through a longer and slower cooking process that would otherwise dry out the meat if it were not for the use of liquid. The liquid, however, is brought up to two-thirds of the height of the item being braised, allowing the exposed top to caramelize. Turning the item once or twice will allow for a more even caramelization.

Braised foods (i.e., osso bucco) are usually seared prior to braising in order to obtain a richer color and flavor. Unlike boiling, braised foods cook partly submerged in liquid (around ½–⅔ full). Some foods are braised without searing (i.e., fish, endive, and celery).

Braising is started on the stove and finished covered in a 350°F oven.

BRAISING TIPS:

Turn the product for more even cooking. Braised foods are done when a fork can be inserted without *any* resistance.

Some liquids used in braising: water, wine, beer, sauce, stock.

FRYING

While fried foods may not be as trendy as they once were, enjoying them in moderation can still be a delightful part of a balanced lifestyle.

For those who are mindful of their fat intake—whether it's saturated, unsaturated, or trans fats—there are ways to enjoy frying while keeping it light. When done thoughtfully, you can minimize the amount of fat absorbed into your favorite dishes, allowing you to savor the flavors you love without compromise.

FRYING TIPS:

Make sure a good quality oil is used.

Make sure the temperature of the oil is correct. Generally, 350°F is right for most products, but not all. Any item with sugar in it may require a lower temperature (i.e., honey dipped chicken, coconut shrimp) as the sugar will brown before the item is cooked.

Slowly lower the food item into the oil to prevent splashing. Always drop food away from you to prevent getting burned.

Remove item from fat when desired doneness is achieved. If an item needs further cooking but the color is dark enough, finish it

in a 350°F oven. Never microwave fried foods, as the steam effect softens the crispiness of fried foods.

Drain all fried foods on clean paper towels. Fried foods should be cooked as needed or will lose their crispness after sitting for just 10 minutes.

POACHING

This is when an item is completely submerged in a court bouillon (which includes water, bouquet garni, vinegar, and mirepoix—50% onions, 25% carrots, 25% celery), which has been brought to 180°F prior to adding the food. The court bouillon imparts some aromatic flavor to the dish.

POACHING TIPS:
Bring the seasoned liquid to poaching temperature prior to adding any food.

SHALLOW POACHING

This is when products such as fish, shellfish, and chicken are cooked in a covered pan with a small amount of liquid and seasoning. Typically, but not always, this liquid is made up of shallots, butter, wine, vinegar, salt, pepper, and fresh herbs. Unlike poaching, in this case, the food is not submerged in liquid.

It is usually reduced and finished with cream or just butter and strained. The biggest advantage to this method of cooking is the flavor you can retain in the fume or broth after the cooking. Garnishes such as tomato, herbs or mushrooms can be added for additional flavor and color.

SHALLOW POACHING TIPS:
This is best when started on the stove, covered, and finished in the oven.

The broth left in the pan is very flavorful and should be finished with butter or cream to be used as the sauce.

SIMMERING

This is one of the most important cooking methods. Stocks, soups, sauces, and stews are made using the simmering method. The liquid while simmering is stronger than poaching and softer than boiling at 208°F. It gently extracts flavor without breaking up the ingredients and causing cloudiness. It cooks with little reduction and has less of a chance of scorching because of the lower temperature.

STEAMING

This is clean, simple, and nutritious. When steaming food, no flavor is added to it, and none is taken away. It is excellent for vegetables as they retain more nutrients than when boiled. Fish can also be steamed with excellent results, however you will need a flavorful sauce to begin with, as you will not yield any juice for sauce making.

Steaming food can be done on the stove in a double stacked pan with water in the bottom, or in a perforated pan and cover.

STEAMING TIPS:

Herbs and spices can be added to the broth, which can make the food more fragrant.

STEWING

This is very similar to braising, except the food is completely submerged in liquid. Searing is only necessary when color and taste from caramelization are desired.

STEWING TIPS:

Using the proper amounts of liquid and cooking the product until it is tender are the two critical aspects of stewing and braising. If too much liquid is used, the flavor extracted from the item will be diluted. If the item is underdone, it will be too tough to chew.

ESSENTIAL KNIFE CUTS

BASIC CUTS

Below is a summary of the essential knife cuts we use at BLACKBARN and at home. Each cut has a specific purpose, whether for cooking efficiency, aesthetics, or texture. Mastering these cuts can significantly enhance a dish's presentation and consistency.

CHOP: A basic cut used for rough or rustic cuts, where uniformity is not as crucial. It involves cutting food into roughly similar-sized pieces.

DICE: A cut that produces small, even cubes. There are three main sizes:
Large Dice: Approximately ¾-inch cubes.
Medium Dice: About ½-inch cubes.
Small Dice: Around ¼-inch cubes.

MINCE: A very fine, small chop often used for garlic, ginger, or herbs, where the pieces are smaller than a small dice.

SPECIALTY CUTS

BATONNET: Slightly larger than julienne, producing rectangular sticks, typically ¼-inch by ¼-inch and about 2 to 3 inches long. This is often a precursor to dicing.

CHIFFONADE: A technique for leafy herbs or greens, where leaves are stacked, rolled, and then sliced into thin ribbons. Common with basil or spinach.

JULIENNE: A cut where food is sliced into thin, matchstick-like strips, about $1/8$-inch thick and 2 inches long. Often used for carrots or celery in salads.

OBLIQUE/ROLL CUT: Often used for root vegetables, this technique involves cutting at an angle, rolling the ingredient after each cut, resulting in a triangular or wedge shape.

PARISIENNE: Used to create spherical shapes from fruits or vegetables using a melon baller. This round cut enhances presentation, adding elegance to dishes and garnishes.

RONDELLE: A round or circular cut, typically used on cylindrical vegetables like carrots or cucumbers.

MEET OUR CHEFS

CHEFS BRIAN FOWLER AND ISRAEL REYES

BLACKBARN, NoMad District, New York

Because BLACKBARN is a very large restaurant with many moving parts, the administrative end of the business requires most of my time and energy on a daily basis. If I devoted too much time to the kitchen, BLACKBARN would immediately feel the effects and suffer as a result. This is the reason I set up BLACKBARN so there would be executive chefs who could dedicate their entire day to running the kitchen. Then, by dinner service, when things really start rocking at BLACKBARN, I can step away from the phone or computer and cook to my heart's desire.

I believe another critical component to the success of BLACKBARN is my relationship with the chefs. I find it extremely important that we are on the same page when it comes to food conceptualization and implementation. As owner, it is my responsibility to create a vision and share my roadmap for success. But I depend on my chefs to be the collaborators in that effort. If I found there was a disconnect in our thinking, I'm certain there would be either inconsistencies or turmoil, or both.

In 2015 when we opened BLACKBARN, Chef Matteo Bergamini was the executive chef. He was born and trained in Italy and had some excellent training in French restaurants throughout New York City. For five years, especially during the pandemic, Chef Matteo worked with me to develop many of our signature dishes that we serve today and that you'll find throughout the pages of this book. He also developed and trained his rising star Sous Chef, Brian Fowler.

When we reopened BLACKBARN after the pandemic, Brian Fowler was ready. It didn't take long for him to step into the shoes of Chef Matteo, who found alternative employment during our closure. Today, Chef Brian and his Executive Sous Chef, Israel Reyes, are outstanding as they run our day-to-day kitchen operation.

Early in his culinary career, Brian attended Cordon Bleu School in Miami. After graduating from school, he honed his skills at various French, Italian, and Japanese restaurants in both Miami and New York. Since we were both raised on Long Island, we came from a similar culture and pedigree which made working together an absolute joy. When Chef Brian and I would sit down to revise menus for the upcoming season, we each came to the table with fresh ideas. As we shared them with one another,

one idea inspired another and by the end of our meeting, we'd get up from the table excited to incorporate our new creations.

As chefs at BLACKBARN, there isn't any ego or false pride in any dish. It's complete collaboration, teamwork, and passion. And because Chef Brian cannot run the kitchen without a strong team, Chef Israel Reyes brings an essential positive "can do" attitude and motivates the team while sourcing seasonal ingredients and creating specials. Chef Israel, born and raised in Puebla, Mexico, immigrated to the United States when he was fifteen, hopeful for a better life and better opportunities. When he came to us, he was committed and ready to work. As most chefs who begin in the industry, he started as our dishwasher and worked his way up the ladder, becoming one of our leading chefs.

Israel's culinary passion began in his mother's kitchen, watching her spend hours preparing traditional Mexican dishes for friends and family. She made every part of the meal with her hands, completely from scratch, showing her son what the joy of cooking really looks like. From a young age, Israel can remember his mother teaching him how to make traditional mole, barbacoa, the proper way to prepare rice, season soups, and make fresh homemade tortillas on the comal. Still to this day, his mother will remind him that, "*Cualquier cosas que prepares con pasión y amor siempre sabrá delicioso.*" Translation: Anything you prepare with passion and love will always taste better. Israel instills this same ideal when cooking at home for his family or for our guests at BLACKBARN. Chef Israel often tells me what he loves most about being a chef at our restaurant is watching our guests smile while enjoying their delicious meal and then thanking him as they leave, happy, content, and satisfied.

CHEF MARCOS CASTRO AND PASTRY CHEF KERRY HAGERTY

BLACKBARN
Hudson Valley,
New York

Since I spend the majority of my time at BLACKBARN in New York's NoMad district, it's important to know we have two outstanding chefs capable of delivering the same high-quality standards from a restaurant ninety miles away. I proudly admit, Chef Marcos Castro and Pastry Chef Kerry Hagerty are two extremely talented individuals who run the show at our BLACKBARN location in Hudson Valley. My business partner Tom Struzzieri cannot say enough great things about their talent, commitment, and integrity. Our core menu at both restaurants is much the same, and is based on guest favorites, which we call our "signature dishes." Chef Marcos and Chef Kerry then have the freedom to develop those dishes further, depending on the season.

In 2009, Chef Marcos arrived in New York to attend The Culinary Institute of America. After graduation, he moved away to build his resumé, working for some of the best and busiest hotels and catering facilities around. It wasn't long until he returned to Hudson Valley where he

became passionate about the ability to source the best local and seasonal ingredients this beautiful part of New York had to offer.

From a very young age, Chef Marcos knew he wanted to be a chef. Having the ability to feed people professionally allowed him a golden opportunity to touch people's lives with something that he created especially for them. Cooking also allowed him the chance to turn an activity that one must do every day into something passionate that can be enjoyed and shared with loved ones. His style of cooking is very seasonal with a strong emphasis on local and sustainable ingredients. In his humble opinion, farm fresh is always the way to go. And with so many farmers' markets, bakeries, local cheese makers, breweries, and wineries surrounding Hudson Valley, there is no need to go very far for the best ingredients.

Then there's our incredible pastry chef, Kerry, who was born and raised in the Hudson Valley, and attended The Culinary Institute of America. Following her studies, she worked at such notable establishments as the Scottsdale Arizona Princess Resort, the historic Beacon Inn in New York, and at The New York Foundling, a charitable organization servicing the five boroughs of New York, where Kerry planned and prepared meals for underprivileged youth.

Kerry attributes her love of baking to her mother, whom she says, "Always brought love and warmth to other people from her kitchen." It is also genuinely inspired and perhaps inherited from her grandfather, who happened to be an executive chef at The Ship Lantern Inn, in Milton, New York, one of the oldest and most prominent restaurants in Hudson Valley.

In 2013, Kerry accepted the position of Pastry Chef at BLACKBARN in Hudson Valley, where she specialized in wedding cakes and pastries. Through hard work, natural talent, and an unwavering dedication, we promoted her to Executive Pastry Chef in 2016.

Today, with her extraordinary flair for flavor and design, Kerry continues to create beautiful, delectable desserts for us as well as exquisite wedding and special occasion cakes, proving she truly can do it all.

BRUNCH

Nothing sets the stage for an enjoyable weekend of rest and relaxation better than a good brunch. In Saugerties, brunch at BLACKBARN means experiencing Chef Marcos's chorizo empanadas with a refreshing mocktail overlooking the cascading waterfall or dining in front of the warm hearth with a cheesy Croque Madame and a crisp, fruity Bellini. Our brunch items do very well year-round at both our locations. We just keep them seasonal by infusing our central dishes with the fresh ingredients we have on hand. For me personally, weekend brunches allow the opportunity to sleep in, get that workout in, have a free afternoon to stroll, shop, and curl up on the couch, leaving me refreshed and ready for a light dinner. Another benefit to brunch is if you like to get to bed early, you're not up late cleaning the dishes. Aside from the tranquil setting of BLACKBARN, either in Saugerties or NoMad, my favorite place to enjoy brunch is by the water while warmed by the sun with a gentle breeze and the sounds of the shore. If I cannot find that, as long as the champagne is chilled, I'll be just fine.

JUICES AND BEVERAGES

Almost every day when I get up, I'll make a fresh juice for my wife and myself, not only because we enjoy the taste but also because of its health benefits. I know I am not alone in seeking out a healthier lifestyle without giving up those little indulgences we all crave. "Everything in moderation," as they say, seems to be the best motivator for me. So, when Jennifer and I travel or go out for brunch, we'll find some good juice shots to start our day. The following recipes are our most popular varieties at the restaurant. When at home, I'll make enough for two days while saving on cleanup time.

CARROT MIXER

MAKES 3½ QUARTS

4 large carrots
2 cups passion fruit juice
½ pineapple, trimmed, cored, and sliced
3 oranges, peeled

Add the carrots, passion fruit juice, pineapple, and oranges to a juicer. Serve chilled or over ice.

BEETROOT JUICE

MAKES 6 CUPS

2 large beetroots
2 pieces ginger, thumb sized, peeled
1 pineapple, peeled and sliced
½ lemon, peeled
4 tablespoons honey

Add the beetroots, ginger, pineapple, lemon, and honey to a juicer. Serve chilled or over ice.

GREEN JUICE

MAKES 8 CUPS

2 bunches kale, roughly chopped
2 large lemons, peeled and quartered
1 piece ginger, thumb sized
4 cucumbers, roughly chopped
2 large green apples, roughly chopped
1 stalk celery, roughly chopped

Add the kale, lemons, ginger, cucumber, apples, and celery to a juicer. Serve chilled or over ice.

BENEFITS OF JUICING

Fruit and vegetable juices offer a wide array of health benefits, making them a valuable addition to a balanced diet. They are rich in essential vitamins, minerals, and antioxidants that help boost the immune system, support digestion, and improve overall health. For instance, citrus juices like orange and lemon are high in vitamin C, which strengthens the immune system and promotes skin health.

Vegetable juices, such as those made from spinach, kale, and carrots, are packed with nutrients like iron, potassium, and beta-carotene, which contribute to healthy blood circulation, vision, and skin. These juices also provide a convenient way to increase your daily intake of vegetables, especially for those who struggle to eat enough servings in solid form.

Moreover, juicing helps in detoxifying the body by flushing out toxins and improving liver function. It also aids in hydration, as fruits and vegetables have high water content. Additionally, consuming juice can be an energy booster, as the natural sugars and nutrients in fruits and vegetables provide a quick, healthy energy source. However, it's important to consume juices in moderation and opt for fresh, homemade versions to avoid added sugars and preservatives often found in store-bought options.

BLOODY MARY
WITH HOMEMADE HOT SAUCE

MAKES 10 CUPS

BLOODY MARY MIX
2 quarts tomato juice
7 tablespoons tomato paste
1 tablespoon paprika
4 tablespoons Homemade
      Hot Sauce (page 92)
3 tablespoons celery salt
11 tablespoons fresh
      horseradish
5½ tablespoons
      Worcestershire sauce
¾ cup orange juice
½ cup lime juice
1 tablespoon black pepper
¼ tablespoon chipotle in
      adobo, optional

FOR 1 COCKTAIL
1 ounce premium vodka
Garnish: Celery stalk or
      dill pickle

Chef Brian really appreciates Bloody Marys, so one day we were motivated to make a Bloody Mary we both enjoy. Here it is! This savory brunch beverage is a little smoky, a little spicy, and is the perfect match for our brunch dishes. Like everything we do at the restaurant, we get inspired to take a classic drink or dish and infuse it with a slight element of delight. For this recipe, feel free to substitute the vodka with tequila for a Bloody Maria.

To make the Bloody Mary Mix: Add the tomato juice, tomato paste, paprika, Hot Sauce, celery salt, horseradish, Worcestershire, orange juice, lime juice, black pepper, and chipotle in adobo in a pitcher. Mix well and pour into an airtight container. Store in the refrigerator for up to 1 week.

To make the cocktail: Add 1 cup of the Bloody Mary Mix and vodka to a cocktail shaker. Shake vigorously and pour into a pint glass filled with ice. Garnish with a celery stalk or dill pickle and serve.

HOMEMADE HOT SAUCE

MAKES 8 CUPS

1 pound sweet cherry peppers,
  seeded, cut in half
1 Spanish onion, peeled and
  large diced
1 red bell pepper, large diced
2 cloves garlic, peeled and
  smashed
1 tablespoon juniper berries
½ tablespoon allspice
2 star anise
1 tablespoon black
  peppercorns
8 sprigs fresh thyme
2 bay leaves
2 cups sugar
1 cup kosher salt
5 cups white wine vinegar
8 guajillo peppers, soaked for
  24 hours, seeded, cut in half
4 ancho peppers, soaked for
  24 hours, seeded, cut in half

Not long after we opened BLACKBARN, whenever a guest would ask for hot sauce, we would hand them Tabasco. Naturally, most restaurants have Tabasco as it's a popular and familiar condiment. When we began working on our brunch menu, we asked ourselves why don't we come up with our own hot sauce? After spending time developing the recipe, we were extremely pleased with the results and so were our guests. Our cherry pepper hot sauce bursts with a vibrant red hue, reflecting its bold, zesty flavors. We combine sweet and tangy notes with a spicy kick, making it both flavorful and fiery. Whenever you want to add a little kick to a dish, simply add this hot sauce.

Preheat the oven to 375°F.

Add the cherry peppers, onions, bell pepper, and garlic to a lined baking sheet and roast in the oven for 18 minutes. While roasting, add the juniper berries, allspice, star anise, and black peppercorns to another baking sheet and place in the oven for 7 minutes. Once roasted, add the juniper berries, allspice, star anise, and black peppercorns, along with the thyme sprigs, bay leaves, sugar, salt, and vinegar to a 4-quart saucepot set over high heat. Bring the pot to a boil. Add the pre-soaked guajillo and ancho peppers, as well as the cherry peppers, onions, bell pepper, and garlic. Remove from the heat. Transfer to a container and allow to cool to under 41°F. Once cool, place in an air-tight container and refrigerate for 2 weeks. After 2 weeks, transfer the fermented contents to a blender and blend on high until smooth. Pass the purée through a fine mesh strainer. Return the sauce to an airtight container and store in the refrigerator up to 1 month.

BREAKFAST PASTRIES

ALMOND HONEY CROISSANT

WITH LOCAL HONEY AND PEAR-GINGER JAM

MAKES 6 CROISSANTS

CROISSANT DOUGH
⅓ cup lukewarm whole milk
1 teaspoon Catskill Provisions
    (or other local) honey
2 teaspoons active dry yeast
1½ tablespoons melted
    unsalted butter, cooled
1½ tablespoons sugar
2 cups all-purpose flour
1 teaspoon kosher salt
10 tablespoons softened
    unsalted butter
½ cup sliced almonds

EGG WASH
1 large egg
1 tablespoon whole milk

PEAR AND GINGER JAM
1 Hudson Valley (or other
    local) apple, peeled and
    medium diced
4 medium Hudson Valley (or
    other local) pears, peeled
    and medium diced
1 lemon, juiced
1 cup Catskills Provisions
    (or other local) honey
1 teaspoon grated fresh ginger

Prior to attending the Culinary Institute of America, our pastry chef, Kerry, had her first croissant while visiting the school. It was an almond croissant, and it was one of the most delicious pastries she says she ever had. The experience solidified Kerry's choice to go to the CIA. With its layers of dough and butter, this is one flaky croissant. Along with the nutty flavors of almonds and sweet local honey, it's good any time of the day.

To make the Croissant Dough: Add the milk, honey, yeast, and ¼ cup lukewarm water to a bowl. Stir to combine and let sit for 10 minutes to activate the yeast. Stir in the melted butter, sugar, flour, and salt. Mix until a shaggy dough forms, about 5 minutes. Turn the dough out onto a lightly floured work surface and knead for 5 minutes, or until a smooth dough forms. Return the dough to the bowl and cover with plastic wrap. Let sit until doubled in size, about 1 hour. After the first proof (letting the dough rise), turn the dough out onto a lightly floured surface and flatten to expel some of the air. Transfer the dough onto parchment paper and shape it into a rectangle. Fold half of the parchment paper over the dough, forming a 7 × 10-inch rectangle. Use a rolling pin to roll out the dough to fit the 7 × 10-inch rectangle. Cover with plastic wrap and transfer to a sheet pan. Refrigerate overnight.

Place the softened butter onto a new sheet of parchment paper, fold over parchment onto butter and roll out the butter to 6 × 5 inches. Refrigerate overnight as well.

Remove the dough and butter from the refrigerator and let sit until both are pliable. Place the dough onto a lightly floured work surface. Place the butter onto one half of the dough. Fold the other half of the dough on top of the butter (resembling a book). Press the edges of the dough all the way around to lock in the butter. Wrap in plastic wrap and refrigerate for 30 minutes.

(Continued)

Remove the dough from the refrigerator and place onto a lightly floured surface. Roll to approximately 16 inches. Brush any excess flour off the dough. Fold both ends of the dough to meet at the middle. Then fold the ends together again. Cover again in plastic wrap and refrigerate for 1 hour.

Place dough onto a lightly floured work surface. Roll dough out to 16 inches. Brush off excess flour. Fold one end of dough to halfway point. Fold other half of dough on top. Plastic wrap and refrigerate for 1 hour.

Remove the dough from the refrigerator and place onto a lightly floured surface. Roll to about ¼-inch thickness, making sure to place the dough back into the refrigerator if the dough gets too warm. Plastic wrap and refrigerate for 30 minutes.

Remove the dough from the refrigerator and place onto a lightly floured surface. Cut the dough into 6 even triangles. With the point of the croissant facing away from you, roll the dough towards the tip. Place the rolled croissants onto a parchment lined sheet pan, making sure the tip of the croissants is under the dough, so they do not unravel while proofing. Cover with plastic wrap and proof until doubled in size.

Preheat the oven to 375°F.

Make the Egg Wash: Add the eggs and milk to a bowl and whisk until incorporated.

Brush the Egg Wash over the dough and sprinkle with the sliced almonds. Bake for 20 to 30 minutes, or until cooked through. Remove and let cool.

While the croissants are baking, make the Pear-Ginger Jam: Add the apple, pears, lemon juice, and ½ cup water to a saucepot over medium heat. Let simmer for 15 minutes, or until the fruit is tender. Stir in the honey and ginger. Simmer for another 10 minutes. Remove from the heat and cool in the refrigerator until needed.

To serve: Cut a cooled croissant lengthwise, spoon the Pear-Ginger Jam over the top (or on the side) and serve.

CARAMELIZED CROISSANT
WITH ESPRESSO PASTRY CREAM

MAKES 8 ROUND CROISSANTS

Croissant Dough (page 96)
Egg Wash (page 98)

ESPRESSO PASTRY CREAM
1½ cups whole milk
1½ cups heavy cream
1 vanilla bean, scraped
2 large eggs
3 egg yolks
¾ cup sugar
4 tablespoons cornstarch
3 tablespoons coffee extract

Kerry wanted to make something that was challenging but able to be replicated at home. She says, "It's hard to think of a better breakfast than a croissant," and I have to agree. This croissant is just the right amount of crunchy with its caramelized exterior while the espresso pastry cream gives it an extra kick to get your morning started.

Preheat the oven to 375°F.

Bake the croissants according to the previous recipe but roll into rounds. While they're baking, make the Espresso Pastry Cream: Add the milk, heavy cream, and vanilla bean to a saucepot over medium heat. Whisk to incorporate. Add the eggs, yolks, sugar, and cornstarch to a bowl and whisk until incorporated. Bring the milk mixture to a boil. Once boiling, remove from the heat and temper half of the hot milk into the bowl with the eggs. Whisk in the rest of the milk mixture. Return the mixture to the pot over medium heat and whisk constantly until thickened. Remove from the heat, add the coffee extract, and place the pot on top of an ice bath to cool immediately.

To serve: Place the Espresso Pastry Cream into a piping bag, pipe onto the croissant rounds, and serve.

ORANGE CARDAMOM CINNAMON BUNS

MAKES 12 BUNS

DOUGH
10 tablespoons unsalted butter
1½ cups whole milk
4½ teaspoons active dry yeast
5 cups all-purpose flour
1 teaspoon kosher salt
1 teaspoon ground cardamom
⅓ cup sugar
1 large egg
2 oranges, zested

FILLING
½ cup softened unsalted butter
1 tablespoon ground cinnamon
1 cup dark brown sugar
1 orange, zested

GLAZE
¼ cup heavy cream
½ cup dark chocolate

Kerry shares that throughout her childhood, her mom would always make cinnamon rolls for breakfast. She'd wake up to the sweet smell of caramelizing brown sugar and cinnamon. Here, she wanted to make something that captured that feeling but with the addition of cardamom and orange.

Add the butter to a saucepot over medium heat. Melt the butter until it turns brown, about 10 minutes. Remove the browned butter and set aside to cool to room temperature. Add the milk to the saucepot and warm, about 2 minutes, or until just warm. Remove the pot from the heat, add the yeast, and stir. Let stand for 5 minutes.

Add the flour, salt, cardamom, and sugar to the bowl of a mixer with dough attachment. Add the milk mixture, egg, and orange zest. Mix until combined. Add 6 tablespoons of the browned butter, reserving the remaining butter for later. Mix for 5 minutes. Place the dough into an oiled bowl, cover with plastic wrap, and let sit at room temperature for 1 hour.

While dough is resting, make the filling by adding the butter, cinnamon, and brown sugar to a mixing bowl and mix until combined.

Once the dough has doubled in size, place onto a floured work surface. Roll the dough out to ½-inch thickness (and approximately 6 × 12 inches). Spread the filling evenly onto the dough. Sprinkle the orange zest evenly on top of the filling. Next, roll the dough towards yourself until even. Cut in half, then cut each half into thirds. Place the buns on a parchment lined sheet pan. Cover and rest until doubled in size.

Preheat the oven to 350°F.

(Continued)

Bake the buns for 25 to 30 minutes, or until a toothpick inserted into the center comes out clean. Remove and brush with the remaining browned butter. While the buns cool, make the glaze.

To make the Glaze: Add the cream to a saucepot over medium-high heat and bring to a boil. Remove and pour the hot cream into a mixing bowl. Add the chocolate and stir until combined with the cream. Pour over the cooled buns and serve.

APPETIZERS

AVOCADO TOAST
WITH LEMON DRESSING

SERVES 4 TO 6

LEMON DRESSING
MAKES 1 CUP
¼ cup fresh lemon juice
¾ cup olive oil
1 teaspoon sea salt

AVOCADO TOAST
3 avocados, chopped
½ red onion, peeled and
    small diced
1 jalapeño, small diced
2 tablespoons chopped fresh
    cilantro
1 lime, juiced
Sea salt and fresh cracked
    black pepper, to taste
4 to 6 slices toasted
    sourdough bread
2- to 3-ounce piece of
    Ricotta Salata

This simple dish is such a perfect brunch dish. It's light, healthy, satisfying, and delicious. There really isn't a standard recipe for this; everyone has their own version. I feel what sets ours apart is we use our house-made sourdough that we press, season, bake, and finish with a grating of Ricotta Salata. I find it complements all the other ingredients so nicely. Our Avocado Toast is also delicious with a fried sunny-side up egg on top.

Begin by making the Lemon Dressing: Add the lemon juice, olive oil, and salt to a small to medium bowl. Whisk vigorously until combined. Refrigerate in an airtight container until ready to serve. The dressing will last in the refrigerator up to 1 week.

Using a medium-sized bowl, add ¼ cup of the Lemon Dressing along with the avocados, onion, jalapeño, cilantro, and lime juice and mix until creamy. Season to taste with salt and pepper. Chill in the refrigerator until ready to serve, up to 2 days.

To serve, evenly portion the avocado mixture on top of each toasted sourdough slice and evenly grate the Ricotta Salata over the avocado.

CHARRED GEM LETTUCE
WITH GREEN GODDESS DRESSING

SERVES 4 TO 6

GREEN GODDESS DRESSING
MAKES 3½ CUPS
2 avocados, pitted and peeled
1 cup Labneh (see Ingredients and Pantry)
5 anchovy fillets
6 chives
1 sprig tarragon
2 sprigs mint
½ jalapeño, deseeded and minced
1 lime, juiced
½ cup orange juice
Kosher salt and fresh cracked black pepper, to taste

CHARRED GEM LETTUCE
4 heads gem lettuce, split in half
4 tablespoons olive oil
2 cups Green Goddess Dressing

When Chef Brian told me he wanted to put Charred Lettuce on the menu, I said, "You want to do what?" It sounds crazy, but it is so good. The lettuce is still sweet and juicy, a little warm and a little cold with a bit of crunch from the breadcrumbs, and the creamy dressing brings it all together. Historically, I'm not a big salad eater, but I love this salad and enjoy it often.

To make the Green Goddess Dressing: Add the avocado, Labneh, anchovy, chives, tarragon, mint, jalapeño, lime juice, and orange juice to a food processor. Blend until smooth. Season with salt and pepper and transfer to an airtight container in the refrigerator until ready to use, up to 1 week.

Preheat the outdoor grill to 500°F.

Season the open-face side of the split gem lettuce heads with olive oil, salt, and pepper. Place them facedown on the hottest portion of the grill and char for 2 minutes at most. Remove from the grill and place on individual plates. Drizzle the desired amount of Green Goddess Dressing on top of each salad and serve.

BLUE CORN "JOHNNY CAKES"

SERVES 4 TO 6

SELF-RISING FLOUR
MAKES 1 CUP

1 cup all-purpose flour
1½ teaspoons baking powder
½ teaspoon kosher salt

**BLOODY BUTCHER
CORNMEAL**
MAKES 1 CUP

1 cup Bloody Butcher
    cornmeal
1½ tablespoons baking
    powder
½ teaspoon kosher salt

JOHNNY CAKES

1 cup Self-Rising Flour
1 cup Bloody Butcher
    Cornmeal (see Ingredients
    and Pantry)
1 tablespoon packed brown
    sugar
2 large eggs
¾ cup buttermilk
⅓ cup water
4 tablespoons unsalted butter
    (or bacon grease)

GARNISH

1½ cups ricotta
1 cup honeycomb or ¼ cup
    elderflower honey
Fresh strawberries,
    raspberries, blueberries,
    and blackberries

The origin of the American Johnny Cake is a bit controversial with various claims on its roots, but the best version is the Hoe Cake. As the story goes, back in the day, the cakes were cooked in bacon grease on a garden hoe over a fire. Chef Brian has taken a family recipe and perfected it by using stone ground blue corn meal that's cooked in whole butter in a cast iron skillet, resulting in a cake that's crunchy on the outside and soft on the inside. Then he'll add a generous piece of local honeycomb, fresh berries, and whipped cream. It's one of our best-selling brunch items and definitely worth making at home.

To make the Self-Rising Flour: Add the flour, baking powder, and salt to a medium bowl. Mix well and transfer to an airtight container and store until ready to use, for up to 1 month.

To make the Bloody Butcher Cornmeal: Add the cornmeal, baking powder, and salt to a medium bowl. Mix well and transfer to an airtight container and store until ready to use, for up to 1 month.

To make the Johnny Cakes: Add the Self-Rising Flour, Bloody Butcher Cornmeal, and brown sugar to a medium mixing bowl. Mix well. Gradually whisk in the eggs, buttermilk, and water. Continue to mix until no lumps are present.

Add the butter (or grease) to a cast-iron skillet over medium-high heat. When the butter has started foaming, spoon the batter into approximately 2-inch-wide discs. Cook one until golden brown and crispy, about 2 to 3 minutes. Flip it over and repeat.

Evenly distribute the "Johnny Cakes" onto individual serving plates. Spoon a dollop of ricotta on top of each cake. Garnish with honeycomb (or honey) and fresh berries and serve.

MAINE LOBSTER ROLL
WITH CHIMICHURRI AIOLI AND ROASTED TOMATOES

MAKES 4 TO 6 LOBSTER ROLLS (OR SERVES 12 AS HORS D'OEUVRES)

MAINE LOBSTER
3 (1¼-pound) live Maine lobsters

AIOLI
1 egg yolk
¼ teaspoon kosher salt
2 cloves garlic, peeled and minced
¼ cup olive oil
2 teaspoons fresh lemon juice

LITE CHIMICHURRI
3 tablespoons red wine vinegar
2 tablespoons olive oil
1 clove garlic, peeled
½ teaspoon crushed red pepper flakes
3 tablespoons fresh cilantro leaves
3 tablespoons fresh basil leaves
3 tablespoons fresh Italian flat leaf parsley leaves

ROASTED TOMATOES
1 quart cherry tomatoes (about 25 tomatoes, depending on size)
1 shallot, peeled and thinly sliced
2 sprigs fresh thyme leaves, chopped
2 cloves garlic, peeled and thinly sliced
Kosher salt and fresh cracked black pepper, to taste

Lobster rolls, if you're not familiar, are a popular summer item along the coastal towns of the Northeast. Because they can be quite expensive, it's disappointing when I order one and quickly find out after a bite or two that the lobster is overcooked, or the dressing is plain mayonnaise. At BLACKBARN, we're proud of our lobster roll and find it's worth the few extra steps to make it. We'll make them as both hors d'oeuvres and lunch-size sandwiches. Best of all, you can enjoy one while on a Hudson River boat tour, because everything is better on the water, don't you agree?

To prepare the lobster: Add 1 gallon of cold water to a medium stockpot over high heat. Once boiling, add the lobster. Reduce the heat to medium-high and cook the lobster for 7 minutes. Remove the lobster and immediately submerge in an ice water bath. Crack open the lobster and separate the meat from the shell, discarding the shells. Medium dice the lobster meat and refrigerate.

To make Aioli: Add the egg yolk, salt, and garlic to a small bowl and mix well with a whisk. Slowly incorporate the olive oil a few drops at a time while whisking until very smooth. Add the lemon juice and whisk until completely emulsified. Set aside until ready to use.

To make the Lite Chimichurri: Add the vinegar, olive oil, garlic, and crushed red pepper to a blender. Mix until smooth. Add the cilantro, basil, and parsley to a mixing bowl. Add the mixture from the blender to the bowl and mix well. Set aside until ready to use.

To make the Roasted Tomatoes: Preheat the oven to 350°F. Add the tomatoes, shallot, thyme, and garlic to a small ovenproof bowl and mix to combine. Season with salt and pepper and roast for 25 minutes. Remove and set aside until ready to use.

(Continued)

OTHER
Fresh brioche rolls

To assemble, lightly brown the brioche rolls. Mix equal parts Lite Chimichurri and Aioli, then add the lobster meat and mix. Fill the roll with the mixture and top with the Roasted Tomatoes to serve.

AN EXTENSION OF OUR OUR ROOTS, BLACKBARN HUDSON VALLEY

MAINE LOBSTER FISHING

Catching Maine lobster on the East Coast, particularly in the cold, clear waters off the coast of Maine, is a tradition deeply rooted in New England's maritime heritage. The process of lobster fishing is both an art and a science, requiring skill, knowledge of the sea, and respect for the marine environment. Lobstermen (and women) typically use small boats, often passed down through generations, to set and haul traps along the rocky coastlines. These traps, or "pots," are baited with herring or other fish to lure lobsters inside.

Once a lobster is caught, it is measured to ensure it meets strict size regulations—only those within a specific size range can be kept to maintain sustainable lobster populations. Larger lobsters, often referred to as "breeders," are released back into the ocean to help sustain the species. Lobstering is regulated by state and federal laws, including quotas and seasons, to protect the lobster population and the livelihoods of those who depend on it.

The catch is then sold to local markets, seafood distributors, and restaurants like BLACKBARN, where lobster becomes a key ingredient in our beloved dishes like our Maine Lobster Roll, which is filled with sweet, tender lobster meat.

MAINS

CORN FLAKE CRUSTED FRENCH TOAST

WITH CARAMELIZED APPLES AND CRÈME ANGLAISE

SERVES 4 TO 6

CARAMELIZED APPLES
MAKES 3 CUPS

½ cup brown sugar

1 tablespoon cinnamon powder

3 Gala apples, peeled and cut into thin wedges

2 tablespoons unsalted butter

½ cup brandy

¼ cup maple syrup

CRÈME ANGLAISE
MAKES 3 CUPS

½ cup sugar

3 egg yolks

1 cup heavy cream

1 cup whole milk

½ vanilla bean, scraped

EGG BATTER
MAKES 5 CUPS

2 cups heavy cream

2 cups whole milk

3 eggs

1 cup sugar

1 vanilla bean, scraped

½ orange, zested

OTHER

5 cups corn flakes

¾ cup all-purpose flour

4 to 6 (2-inch-thick) slices brioche

5 tablespoons unsalted butter

Growing up, I found myself enjoying French toast much more than pancakes, primarily because I discovered a lot more variations to explore in both flavor and texture. This version from our brunch menu is a grown-up version of what I appreciated as a kid, and it's a real crowd-pleaser at the restaurant. The egg batter tastes great on its own, with just a touch of orange and vanilla, but what really sets this dish over the top is the addition of caramelized brandy apples and crunchy cornflakes browned in butter.

Begin by making the Caramelized Apples: Add the brown sugar, cinnamon, and apples to a medium bowl. Toss the apples until they are evenly coated. Add the butter to a 10-inch sauté pan over high heat. Melt the butter until it foams. Add the apples, spreading them evenly across the bottom of the pan. Do not toss or move the apples for at least 2 minutes. This will allow the pan to retain its heat while speeding up the caramelization process. After 2 minutes, give the apples a toss or gently mix with a rubber spatula. Continue to cook for another 3 minutes. Remove the pan from the heat, add the brandy, and return pan to the heat. If using an electric stove, the use of a lighter or match to the pan will set the brandy aflame, aiding in burning off the alcohol. If using a gas stove, a small tilt of the pan towards the flame will do the trick. Continue cooking until the flame inside the pan has dissipated. Add the maple syrup, reduce the heat to medium, and cook for another 4 minutes. Remove from the heat and set aside until ready to use.

To make the Crème Anglaise: Add the sugar and egg yolks to a stand mixer with the whisk attachment (or use a medium bowl with a whisk). Turn the mixer to medium speed and mix until the mixture becomes light yellow (this is called sabayon). Add the heavy cream, milk, and vanilla bean to a 2-quart saucepot over low-medium heat and bring to a simmer. Once simmering, remove from the heat and set beside

(Continued)

BLACKBARN

the stand mixer. Using a rubber spatula, scrape down the sides of the mixing bowl. Pour ⅓ of the milk-cream mixture into the bowl and turn the mixer to low speed. Slowly pour the rest of the hot milk-cream into the bowl and mix for 4 to 6 minutes, or until any bubbles and foam begin to dissipate. Return the egg and cream mixture back to the 2-quart saucepot over low-medium heat. Consistently stir in a figure 8 motion with a rubber spatula. Be sure to move the spatula along the sides and bottom of the pot to ensure nothing is sticking. Continue cooking until mixture evenly coats the back of a spoon or the spatula. Remove from the heat and transfer the mixture to an ice bath. Mix the Crème Anglaise until cool and serve immediately or store in an airtight container in the refrigerator up to 1 week.

To make the Egg Batter: Add the heavy cream, milk, yolks, sugar, vanilla beans, and orange zest to a large bowl. Use a wire whisk to mix until combined. Set aside until ready to use.

To make the Crust: Add the cornflakes to a food processor and blend until the flakes are about the size of peppercorns. Pour them into a flat-bottomed dish. Add the flour, mix again until combined, and set aside.

Dip each slice of brioche into the Egg Batter, soaking each side for at least 30 seconds. Then, dip into the ground cornflakes, generously coating both sides.

Preheat the oven to 340°F.

Add the butter to a 10-inch cast iron skillet over medium heat. Melt the butter until it foams. Add the cornflake-crusted brioche to the skillet and cook each side for 4 minutes. After cooking both sides, place them on a stainless wire roasting rack or a lined baking sheet and put them on the middle rack of the oven for 8 to 10 minutes. When the middle of the French Toast starts to rise, remove it from the oven and place it on a serving platter. Top with the Caramelized Apples and drizzle with the Crème Anglaise. You can leave the Crème Anglaise on the side for dipping.

WAFFLE CROQUE MADAME
WITH CHEESE FONDUE

SERVES 4 TO 6

WAFFLE BATTER
1½ cups warm water, divided
3 tablespoons sugar
1 tablespoon active dry yeast
6 cups whole milk
5 large eggs
3¾ cups all-purpose flour
⅛ teaspoon baking soda
1½ kosher salt
1 stick (8 tablespoons)
    unsalted butter, melted
1½ teaspoons pure vanilla
    extract

CHEESE FONDUE
MAKES 2½ CUPS
2 cups whole milk
Kosher salt and freshly cracked
    black pepper, to taste
¼ teaspoon nutmeg
½ stick (4 tablespoons)
    unsalted butter
¼ cup all-purpose flour
⅔ cup grated Gruyère cheese

OTHER
½ pound thick-cut honey ham
4 to 6 eggs, cooked sunny-
    side up
Fresh chives, chopped, for
    garnish

Everyone in New York City seems to love brunch, including myself. One of my personal favorites when I go for brunch is Croque Madame. The classic dish is comprised of ham and cheesy Mornay sauce layered between white bread, then browned in butter with a thick layer of melted Gruyère on top and crowned with a fried egg. This, and a glass of champagne, is what makes my day. At BLACKBARN, we like to put a twist on the Croque Madame. Instead of white bread we'll add some fresh rosemary and Parmesan cheese to our waffle batter. While the waffle cooks in the iron, the cheese caramelizes and becomes very fragrant. The rest stays classic. What a wonderful dish.

To make the Waffle Batter: Add half of the water along with the sugar, yeast, and milk in a medium mixing bowl. Mix well to combine and let the yeast bloom for at least 10 minutes. Once the yeast has bloomed, separate the eggs and whip the whites to form stiff peaks. Add the flour, baking soda, salt, egg yolks, butter, vanilla, and the remaining water to a large mixing bowl. Mix well and then add the bloomed yeast mixture and stir to incorporate. Fold in the egg whites in 3 parts. Allow the batter to rest for at least 2 hours and up to overnight.

Preheat a waffle iron and grease with non-stick spray or butter. When ready, pour in enough batter to cover the bottom of the iron. Cook until golden brown and remove from the iron. Cut each waffle in half and set aside.

Preheat the oven to 350°F.

To make the Cheese Fondue: Add the milk to a 1-quart saucepot over low-medium heat and bring to a simmer. Season with salt, pepper, and nutmeg.

While waiting for the milk to simmer, add the butter to a 10-inch sauté pan. Melt the butter until it begins to foam. Whisk in the flour,

(Continued)

ensuring no clumps or dry spots and cook for 3 minutes. Add the heated milk into the roux and whisk until well combined. Over low-medium heat, continue to whisk gently until the milk starts to thicken. Cook for another 15 minutes. Strain the sauce through a fine mesh strainer and mix in the cheese until all has melted. Set aside.

Line a baking sheet with foil or parchment paper. Split the waffles horizontally and place one-half of each waffle on the baking sheet and spread a thin layer of the Cheese Fondue on top. Layer with a slice of ham, the other half of the waffle, and another thin layer of Cheese Fondue. Bake for 14 to 16 minutes.

While the waffles are baking, fry the eggs to sunny-side up or the desired temperature.

Once baked, place one layered waffle on each plate. Top with a fried egg, garnish with chopped chives, and serve.

CHORIZO EGG AND CHEESE EMPANADA

SERVES 4 TO 6

EMPANADA DOUGH
MAKES 10 TO 12 (4-INCH)
TORTILLAS

4 cups all-purpose flour
½ teaspoon kosher salt
2 large cage-free egg yolks,
     beaten
1 cup cold water
2 tablespoons diced unsalted
     butter
¾ cup vegetable shortening

SOFRITO
MAKES 2 CUPS

1 small white onion, peeled
     and roughly chopped
1 small red onion, peeled and
     roughly chopped
1 red bell pepper, roughly
     chopped
1 yellow bell pepper, roughly
     chopped
5 cloves garlic, peeled
¼ cup fresh roughly chopped
     cilantro
3 tablespoons olive oil

MOLE SAUCE
MAKES 4 CUPS

2 dried pasilla chilies, cut
     lengthwise, seeds removed
2 dried guajillo chilies, cut
     lengthwise, seeds removed
2 dried ancho chilies, cut
     lengthwise, seeds removed
1 cup chicken stock
⅛ cup white sesame seeds
⅛ cup raw almonds

Chef Marcos believes empanadas are the perfect comfort food and that breakfast is his favorite meal of the day. So, when it comes to a simple and flavor-packed recipe, this one is a home run. This crispy, cheesy, light finger food is perfect for anyone looking for a wow factor that is certain to please.

Begin by making the Empanada Dough: Sift the flour into a mixing bowl. Add the salt, egg yolks, and 1 cup cold water, and gently mix. Cut in the butter and vegetable shortening in small amounts until a dough starts to form. Remove the dough from the bowl and place on a lightly floured surface. Knead the dough until smooth, about 4 minutes. Cover with plastic wrap and refrigerate for at least 1 hour. Remove the dough from the refrigerator and turn out onto a lightly floured surface. Roll out until about $1/8$-inch thick. Cut the dough with a 4-inch ring cutter and set aside until ready to use.

To make the Sofrito: Add the onions, peppers, garlic, and cilantro to a food processor and blend over low speed. While blending, drizzle in the olive oil, being careful not to overmix as you do not want a purée. Remove and transfer the mixture to a small sauté pan over medium heat. Cook until the Sofrito begins to turn translucent, but not brown, about 5 minutes. Remove from the heat and set aside.

To make the Mole Sauce: Add the dried chilies to a large dry pan over high heat and toast while stirring until fragrant, about 3 minutes. Remove the chilies and place in a blender. Add the chicken stock and purée until very smooth. Set aside. Using the same pan for toasting the chilies, add the sesame seeds, almonds, peanuts, cloves, peppercorns, cumin, and star anise. Toast over medium high heat, stirring constantly, until all the ingredients are evenly toasted, about 5 minutes. Add the mixture to the blender with the chilies and purée until smooth. Set aside. Add the olive oil to a medium saucepan over high heat. When the

(Continued)

130   /   BLACKBARN

⅛ cup raw peanuts

2 cloves

3 black peppercorns

½ teaspoon whole cumin seeds

1 star anise

⅛ cup olive oil

½ small white onion, peeled and roughly chopped

5 cloves garlic, peeled and roughly chopped

1 (7-ounce) can plum tomatoes

⅛ cup golden raisins

1 (5-inch) corn tortilla, torn

1 (2-inch) piece baguette, diced

2 tablespoons Mexican bittersweet chocolate, roughly chopped

EMPANADAS

2 tablespoons olive oil + 4 cups for frying, divided

6 ounces ground chorizo sausage

1 medium-sized russet potato, peeled and small diced

¼ cup black beans

2 large cage-free eggs, beaten

¼ cup grated white cheddar cheese

3 tablespoons queso fresco

oil is hot and shimmering, add the onions and garlic and sauté until the vegetables begin to brown, about 4 minutes. Add the tomatoes, raisins, tortillas, and the diced baguette. Add the mixture from the blender and stir until fully incorporated. Add the chocolate and stir until melted. Add back to the blender in small batches and purée until smooth. Set aside.

To make the Empanadas: Add 2 tablespoons of the olive oil to a large saucepan over medium-high heat. When the oil is hot and shimmering, add the chorizo and cook until brown, about 5 minutes. Add the 2 cups of Sofrito and cook until it begins to brown, about 4 minutes. Add the potatoes and cook for another 4 minutes. Add the black beans and eggs. Cook until the eggs are cooked through, about 5 minutes. Fold in the cheese. Remove from the heat and refrigerate the mixture for 30 minutes.

Place ¼ cup of the chilled mixture into the center of the Empanada Dough. Fold in half and crimp the edges with a fork. Set aside. Heat the Mole Sauce in a small saucepan over medium heat and set aside.

Add the remaining 4 cups olive oil to a medium pot over medium-high heat and bring the oil to 350°F. Use a candy or digital thermometer to gauge the temperature. When the oil is at the correct temperature, gently add the Empanadas and fry for 3 minutes on each side, or until golden brown. Remove from the oil and drain on paper towels before serving.

To serve: Spoon the Mole Sauce onto the center of the plate. Place the Empanadas on top of Mole sauce, sprinkle the queso fresco over the empanadas, and serve.

BLACKBARN BURGER
WITH HOMEMADE CHEESE BRIOCHE

SERVES 4

BIGA STARTER
MAKES 3½ TO 4 CUPS
½ teaspoon active dry yeast
1 cup room temperature
    water
2¾ cups all-purpose flour
1 tablespoon olive oil, for
    coating the bowl

CHEESE BRIOCHE
MAKES 10 BUNS
¾ cup heavy cream
5 tablespoons sugar
3 teaspoons fresh yeast
1 cup all-purpose flour
1½ cups Biga Starter
2 teaspoons kosher salt
1 large egg
4 tablespoons softened
    unsalted butter
Egg Wash (page 98)
10 tablespoons freshly grated
    Gruyère cheese

ROASTED PLUM TOMATOES
4 plum tomatoes, split
    lengthwise
2 cloves garlic, peeled
    and sliced
2 basil leaves, torn
1 orange peel
Kosher salt and fresh cracked
    black pepper, to taste

CHIPOTLE-ORANGE
SPICE RUB
MAKES ¾ CUP
1½ tablespoons smoked
    paprika

I take great pride in our burger, which we "engineered." By that I mean every component is carefully selected and made to create one perfect, unforgettable burger. Our burger begins with quality meat. The meat we use is a custom blend of Certified Angus Beef chuck, brisket, and sirloin from our friends at DeBragga & Spitler, who've been providing me excellent meat for more than forty years. You should be able to find Certified Angus Beef at your local market or butcher. To us, the bun is also important. A bun too soft or too hard can be difficult to eat. Same with the cheese. If it isn't sharp enough, you won't taste it. Because sauces are generally on the sweeter side, we like to add a little spice to create balance. I also enjoy a touch of smoke on my burger, which I add with the bacon. You can achieve the same results by placing pre-soaked wood chips on your outdoor grill at home.

To make the Biga Starter: Add the water to a small bowl and stir in the yeast. Let stand for 10 minutes. Add the yeast mixture to the bowl of a stand mixer set at low speed. Add the flour, 1 cup at a time. Mix for 2 to 3 minutes. Transfer the starter to a lightly oiled bowl and cover with plastic wrap. Allow to sit at room temperature for 6 to 8 hours, or until the starter has tripled in size. Place into the desired container and refrigerate until ready to use.

To make the Cheese Brioche: Preheat the oven to 385°F. Add the heavy cream, sugar, and yeast to a medium-sized bowl. Allow the yeast to bloom covered for 15 to 20 minutes, or until small bubbles form on the surface. Add the flour, Biga Starter, salt, egg, and butter, along with the heavy cream and yeast mixture to a stand mixer. Mix until a homogenous dough has formed. Remove the dough from the bowl and transfer to a medium-sized bowl. Cover with plastic wrap and allow to proof for 1 hour. Portion the dough into 10 even pieces. On a lightly floured surface, fold the bottom part of the dough to the middle,

(Continued)

½ tablespoon paprika
1 tablespoon ancho
    chili powder
½ tablespoon chipotle
    chili powder
½ teaspoon cayenne pepper
2½ tablespoons
    granulated onion
2½ tablespoons
    granulated garlic
1½ tablespoons packed dark
    brown sugar
1½ tablespoons dried
    orange zest
1½ tablespoons ground
    coriander
2 teaspoons ground cumin
½ teaspoon thyme
4 teaspoons cocoa powder
1 tablespoon kosher salt
2 teaspoons fresh cracked
    black pepper

BLACKBARN BURGER

8 thick slices bacon
4 (6-ounce) Certified Angus
    Beef patties
Kosher salt, to taste
Fresh cracked black pepper,
    to taste
Chipotle-Orange Spice Rub,
    to taste, optional
Barbecue Sauce (page 138),
    to taste
4 leaves Bibb lettuce
4 thick slices aged
    cheddar cheese
2 jalapeños, small diced
Roasted Plum Tomatoes

followed by the sides, stretching the front of the dough and folding over the center each time. Flip the dough over with a floured hand and tighten the hand to round the dough. Use the pinky sides of your hands to pull the dough towards you while spinning simultaneously. When complete, place on a lined baking sheet. Egg wash the raw dough and sprinkle the Gruyère cheese on top. Bake for 8 minutes, rotate the pan, and bake for another 4 minutes. Remove from the oven and allow to cool before using.

To make the Roasted Plum Tomatoes: Preheat the oven to 325°F. Add the tomatoes, garlic, basil, and orange peel to a medium-sized bowl. Toss until coated and season with salt and pepper. Place the tomatoes on a wire rack with the cut side facing down. Place in the middle rack of the oven and roast for 28 minutes. Remove and peel the skin from the tomatoes and discard. Use immediately or store in an airtight container in the refrigerator up to 1 week.

To make the Chipotle-Orange Spice Rub: Add the paprikas, chili powders, cayenne, granulated onion and garlic, brown sugar, dried orange zest, coriander, cumin, thyme, cocoa powder, salt, and black pepper to a mixing bowl. Mix well until combined, then store in an airtight container until ready to use.*

*Note: To make dried orange zest: Preheat the oven to 250°F. Using a zester or vegetable peeler, remove the outer skin from 2 oranges. Spread the orange peel out on a parchment-lined sheet pan. Allow to dry in the oven until completely dried and brittle, 4 to 5 hours. Grind to a powder with a spice grinder or blender and store in an airtight container until ready to use.

Prepare an outdoor grill to medium-high heat.

Add the bacon and grill on both sides until cooked and crispy, about 6 minutes. Note: You can also cook the bacon in the oven set at 400°F. Simply arrange the bacon on a lined baking sheet and cook until crispy, 8 to 10 minutes.

Season all sides of the beef patties with salt, pepper, and Chipotle-Orange Spice Rub, if using. Place on the grill and cook both sides for 7 minutes for medium. Cook 3 minutes longer for medium-well and 6 minutes longer for well-done. Remove the patties and set them aside.

To build the burger: Split and toast the brioche rolls. Add a lettuce leaf, burger patty, slice of aged cheddar, some jalapeños, a couple Roasted Plum Tomatoes, bacon, Barbecue Sauce, and then crown the burger with the top half of the Brioche and serve.

CERTIFIED ANGUS BEEF

Certified Angus Beef (CAB) is a premium brand of beef renowned for its exceptional quality and flavor. Established in 1978 by a group of Angus cattle ranchers, CAB was the first brand to require beef to meet stringent quality standards beyond those of USDA Prime, Choice, and Select. To earn the CAB label, beef must pass ten rigorous standards, ensuring superior marbling, tenderness, juiciness, and flavor. These standards include a modest or higher degree of marbling, consistent size and appearance, and specific ribeye area and fat thickness requirements. Only about 30 percent of Angus cattle meet these criteria, making Certified Angus Beef a sought-after product in fine dining and gourmet markets. Consumers, like us at BLACKBARN, trust the CAB label for a consistently excellent eating experience, knowing it represents the pinnacle of beef quality. CAB is more than just a brand; it symbolizes the dedication to quality from ranch to table.

BLACKBARN BARBECUE SAUCE

MAKES 4 CUPS

4 tablespoons olive oil
1 large Spanish onion, peeled
    and diced
1 tablespoon chopped garlic
1 teaspoon dried oregano
1 teaspoon dried thyme
1 tablespoon smoked paprika
1 cup tomato paste
¼ cup premium brandy
¼ cup sherry vinegar
5 cups cold water
1 tablespoon chipotle paste
Sea salt and fresh cracked
    black pepper, to taste

Add the oil to a 2- or 3-quart saucepan over medium heat. When the oil is heated, add the onions and cook until translucent, about 4 minutes. Add the garlic and cook for about 2 minutes. Add the oregano, thyme, and paprika, and cook for 2 minutes. Add the tomato paste and cook for 2 minutes. Add the brandy, vinegar, water, and chipotle paste. Reduce the heat to low and simmer until the barbecue sauce has thickened to a ketchup-like consistency, about 30 minutes. Season to taste with salt and pepper. Transfer to an airtight container and refrigerate for up to 2 weeks.

EVENTS

During my time at the Waldorf, where every event was high-profile and VIP-driven, I learned early on that creativity, flexibility, and attention to detail are just as important as the quality of the food. Large wooden signs with gold letters hung in every kitchen at the Waldorf reading:

THE DIFFICULT IS IMMEDIATE . . . THE IMPOSSIBLE TAKES A FEW MINUTES LONGER.

At the Waldorf, nothing was impossible, and I upheld that very philosophy when I opened my own restaurant, where the guest is always right and the possibilities are limitless.

At BLACKBARN, events are essential, not only for the connections they foster but also for the lasting impact they create. Every event is designed with intention, whether a wedding, corporate function, or charity fundraiser. It's not just about sitting down and sharing a meal; it's about creating an experience that resonates long after the event ends. We understand how much detail goes into event planning, which is why our goal is to take the stress out of that process; our events team collaborates closely with each and every client to bring ideas to life.

Whether you want a chef-curated tasting menu, your dream wedding, or a unique hands-on experience in our production kitchen, no idea is too big or too small. We thrive on creating experiential events, whether you want to start the night with a sabered bottle of champagne and make soufflés together or take a cruise on the Hudson River followed by a dock-side dinner.

The BLACKBARN team's mission is to make planning every event seamless and provide bespoke touches to make it memorable. As you plan your next event, remember that the little details make all the difference, and we are at your service. At BLACKBARN, the impossible just takes a little longer, and we bring that "anything is possible" mindset to every event we host.

SIGNATURE COCKTAILS

The neighborhood surrounding BLACKBARN is called North of Madison Square Park or NoMad for short. The area features many fabulous bars and restaurants so great cocktails are not difficult to come by. At our restaurant, we offer craft cocktails that change seasonally just like our menu. According to our guests, we make some amazing drinks. Our bar team curates incredibly tasty, creative cocktails using an array of seasonal ingredients. Try these delicious and popular drinks the next time you entertain.

CLOUD 9

MAKES 1 COCKTAIL

BASE
3½ cups coconut cream
3⅛ cups lime juice
1 bottle (750ml) white rum +
   additional rum, divided
2⅓ cups room temperature
   milk

PINEAPPLE FOAM
1 ounce egg white (about 1
   egg white)
3 ounces pineapple juice

To make the Base: Add the coconut cream, lime juice, and rum to a large container. Whisk until combined and set aside. Add the milk into another large container. Slowly pour the coconut cream mixture into the milk container in a stream to ensure the milk does not curdle. Place in the refrigerator for 2 hours. Remove and, using a coffee filter or cheesecloth, strain the mixture. Note: The first few drops will be cloudy and can be discarded and re-strained to ensure optimal clarification.

To make the Pineapple Foam: Add the egg white and pineapple juice to a cocktail shaker. Dry shake, then add a handful of ice, and shake again. Double strain through a fine mesh strainer and set aside.

To make the cocktail, add 2 ounces of the Base and 1 ounce white rum to a rock glass with one large ice-cube. Top with the Pineapple Foam and serve. Leftover Base should be refrigerated for later use.

BARNYARD TEA

DEHYDRATED LEMON
1 lemon, thinly sliced into
  rounds

BLACK TEA SYRUP
2 cups sugar
2 cups water
2 bags black tea

COCKTAIL
1½ ounces Black Tea Syrup
2 ounces bourbon
1½ ounces lemon juice
5 mint leaves

To make the Dehydrated Lemon: Arrange lemon slices in an air fryer and set to dehydrate at 135°F for 8 hours, flipping them halfway. Set aside until ready for use or seal in an airtight container.

To make the Black Tea Syrup: Add the water and sugar to a 2-quart saucepot over medium-low heat. Bring to a simmer, stirring until the sugar has completely dissolved. Remove from the heat and add the tea bags. Allow to steep for 2 to 5 minutes. Remove the tea bags, transfer to desired container, and chill until ready to use.

Combine 1½ ounces of Black Tea Syrup, the bourbon, and lemon juice in a cocktail shaker. Shake, strain, and pour into a glass over rocks. Garnish with the mint and a dehydrated lemon.

BLUSHING BASIL

COCKTAIL
1 ounce gin
1 ounce pink limoncello
½ ounce simple syrup
1 ounce egg white
3 basil leaves

GARNISH
1 Dehydrated Lemon
(page 150)

Combine the gin, pink limoncello, simple syrup, egg white, and basil leaves in a cocktail shaker. Shake, strain, and pour into a coupe glass.

Garnish with a dehydrated lemon.

HORS D'OEUVRES

GOUGÈRES

MAKES 30 GOUGÈRES

½ cup water
½ cup whole milk
½ cup (1 stick) unsalted butter
¼ teaspoon kosher salt
1 cup all-purpose flour
4 large eggs
3½ cups grated Gruyère
   cheese
Freshly ground black pepper
Freshly ground nutmeg
2 tablespoons freshly grated
   Parmesan cheese

These savory puffs are a great addition to any party. I love the versatility of these as they are the perfect vessel for a variety of different fillings. They are one of the first items we learned to make in culinary school, and I love that we still use this culinary staple at our restaurant.

Preheat the oven to 400°F and line 2 half sheet pans with parchment paper.

Add the water and milk to a saucepot along with the butter and salt over high heat. Bring to a boil, then mix in the flour with a wooden spoon. Continue to mix until the mixture comes together and forms a film on the bottom of the pot, about 2 minutes. Let cool for 1 minute. Beat the eggs into the dough, one egg at a time until each egg is absorbed. Mix in the Gruyère, pepper, and nutmeg. Transfer the mixture to a piping bag. Pipe 30 gougères about 1 tablespoon each in size, with about a half inch of space between each gougère. Sprinkle with Parmesan. Bake for 15 minutes, turn the pan, and bake for another 5 minutes. Remove and set aside to cool before serving.

VICHYSSOISE
WITH HOMEMADE CHICKEN STOCK

SERVES 4 TO 6

**HOMEMADE CHICKEN STOCK
MAKES 2 QUARTS**
2½ pounds chicken bones,
   rinsed under cold water
1 cup chopped yellow onion
½ cup chopped carrots
¼ cup chopped celery
2 cloves garlic, peeled
5 sprigs fresh thyme
6 to 8 Italian flatleaf
   parsley stems
1 bay leaf
3 black peppercorns

VICHYSSOISE
½ pound unsalted butter
1 Spanish onion, peeled and
   medium diced
1 large leek, large diced
Kosher salt, to taste
4 cups Homemade
   Chicken Stock
2 cups heavy cream
3 russet potatoes, peeled and
   large diced
⅛ teaspoon ground nutmeg
Fresh cracked black pepper,
   to taste
4 to 6 teaspoons Siberian
   Osetra caviar

For many years while I was at the Waldorf, Vichyssoise remained on our room service menu. We served the dish in a white China bowl, which was nestled into crushed ice in a silver soup terrine. The presentation was beautiful while refreshing and luxurious at the same time. At BLACKBARN, our thickened and chilled Vichyssoise is made with our homemade chicken stock and garnished with Siberian Osetra caviar because of its salinity and brininess, which pairs beautifully with this soup. We may serve this dish as a soup course at our Chef's Table or simply in a shot glass for a quick, delicious bite at a reception. Either way, Vichyssoise is one of my favorite soups.

To make the Homemade Chicken Stock: Add the chicken bones in a large stockpot along with the onions, carrots, celery, garlic, thyme, parsley stems, bay leaf, and peppercorns. Add enough water to just cover the ingredients. Slowly bring the liquid to a boil over high heat, then immediately reduce the heat to a low simmer. Cook for 3 hours, skimming the top often.

Use a ladle to pass the stock through a fine mesh strainer lined with a double layer of cheesecloth and into a container placed in an ice bath. Do not ladle out any stock from the bottom that contains impurities. Discard the bones and vegetables.

Use the stock immediately or refrigerate in an airtight container for up to 3 days. The stock can also be frozen for longer storage.

To make the Vichyssoise: Add the butter to a 3-quart saucepot over medium-high heat. Melt the butter until it foams. Add the onions, leeks, and season with salt. Cook until the onions are translucent, 4 to 5 minutes. Add the chicken stock, heavy cream, and potatoes. Bring to a boil and then reduce the heat and simmer. Cook until the potatoes are fork tender, 10 to 12 minutes.

(Continued)

Pour half of the soup into a blender and blend until smooth. Repeat with the remaining soup. Season with salt, pepper, and nutmeg. Allow the soup to cool.

Ladle about 1½ cups of the soup into individual soup bowls. Garnish each bowl with a teaspoon of caviar and serve.

CAVIAR

Caviar, one of the world's most luxurious delicacies, is the salt-cured roe (eggs) of sturgeon, particularly from species such as Beluga, Osetra, and Sevruga. This gourmet product has been prized for centuries, often associated with opulence and indulgence. Originating from the Caspian and Black Sea regions, caviar was historically enjoyed by Russian and Persian nobility. Today, it is savored globally in fine dining establishments and at special occasions.

The production of caviar is a meticulous process. Sturgeons, which can take years to mature, are carefully harvested, and their eggs are gently extracted, cleaned, and salted to enhance their natural flavor and preserve them. The quality of caviar is judged by its size, color, flavor, and texture. The most sought-after caviars are known for their large, glossy beads that burst with a delicate, briny flavor, offering a unique and refined tasting experience.

Sustainability has become increasingly important in the caviar industry, as wild sturgeon populations have declined due to overfishing and environmental factors. As a result, much of today's caviar is farmed under controlled conditions, ensuring both the quality of the product and the preservation of sturgeon species. Whether served simply on blinis with crème fraiche, or as part of an elaborate dish, caviar remains a symbol of luxury and culinary excellence.

CRISPY CHICKEN WINGS
WITH CHIPOTLE-ORANGE SPICE RUB

SERVES 4 TO 6

6 cups coconut or avocado oil
for frying
3 pounds chicken wings
6 tablespoons olive oil
1 cup Chipotle-Orange Spice
Rub (page 134)
Kosher salt, to taste
Barbecue Sauce, to taste
(page 138)
Homemade Hot Sauce, to
taste (page 92)

Are you ready for some delicious, finger-lickin' chicken wings? These wings are perfectly seasoned and cooked twice—the first time to get them to "fall off the bone" tender, then chilled and fried to get the skin nice and crisp. At the restaurant, we like to serve the sauce on the side so you can enjoy the wings without sticky fingers. Of course, feel free to toss the wings in the sauce if you prefer.

Preheat the oven to 200°F.

Combine the wings, olive oil, Chipotle-Orange Spice Rub, and salt to taste in a mixing bowl. Toss well until the wings are evenly coated. Spread the wings across a roasting pan and cover with foil. Bake in the oven for 3½ hours. Remove the wings and strain off any juices and oil before allowing to cool. While the wings are cooling, fill a large stockpot with the frying oil and heat over medium heat until the oil reaches 350°F. Use a candy or digital thermometer to check the temperature. Once cool, add the wings in batches into the hot oil and fry for 6 to 8 minutes. Turn the wings a few times to ensure all sides are submerged in oil. Use a kitchen spider or slotted spoon to remove the wings from the oil, allowing the oil to drip off. Serve the wings with a side of Barbecue Sauce and Hot Sauce or simply toss the wings with the desired amount of Barbecue and Homemade Hot Sauce before serving. Note: If you don't intend to fry the wings after removing them from the oven, let the wings cool in the refrigerator and then place them in an airtight container and store in the refrigerator up to 1 week.

MUSHROOM TOAST

SERVES 4

**SAUTÉED MIXED MUSHROOMS
MAKES 3 CUPS**
5 tablespoons olive oil, divided
6 cups of sliced, mixed,
   seasonal mushrooms
   (button, shiitake, baby
   portobello, oyster), divided
3 shallots, peeled and minced
4 sprigs fresh thyme
2 tablespoons sherry vinegar
⅛ cup chopped Italian flat leaf
   parsley
1 tablespoon sea salt, or to
   taste
½ teaspoon fresh cracked
   black pepper

OTHER
2 cups Cheese Fondue
   (page 126)
Lemon Dressing (page 108),
   to taste
2 cups Sautéed Mixed
   Mushrooms
4 thin slices of sourdough
   bread, toasted
½ pound taleggio cheese
1½ cups watercress
½ cup freshly grated
   Parmesan cheese

The backstory on our Mushroom Toast is twofold. It was developed as a vegetarian item to balance the menu and has been a winner since the day we opened. It's a dish guests talk about when they reminisce about their latest meal at BLACKBARN. What happened next has brought greater value to this humble dish. As part of our sustainability program, we partnered with a composting company called AfterLife (see sidebar, page 166). They pick up and compost our organic food waste. Once the compost is ready, they grow mushrooms from it. Lots of mushrooms with great variety. We then purchase the mushrooms at a discount and make our Mushroom Toast as well as other dishes containing mushrooms. It's a win-win!

To make the Sautéed Mixed Mushrooms: Add 1 tablespoon of olive oil to a 12-inch sauté pan over high heat. When the olive oil starts to shimmer, add 2 cups of the mixed mushrooms. Cook for 2 minutes then set the mushrooms aside. Repeat twice with the remaining mushrooms, adding 1 tablespoon of olive oil with each batch.

Add the remaining 2 tablespoons of olive oil to the same pan over medium-high heat. When the olive oil starts to shimmer, add the shallots and sauté for 2 minutes, or until translucent. Add the cooked mushrooms and thyme then add the sherry to deglaze the pan. Continue cooking until all the liquid has evaporated, about 2 minutes. Add the chopped parsley, and season with salt and pepper. Use immediately or cover and refrigerate until ready to serve.

Preheat the oven to 425°F.

Prepare the Cheese Fondue and Lemon Dressing.

(Continued)

164   /   BLACKBARN

Begin layering the Cheese Fondue, Sautéed Mixed Mushrooms, and taleggio onto each slice of bread. Return the sheet to the oven for 8 to 10 minutes. Remove the sheet and transfer the bread slices to a cutting board. Evenly cut 4 pieces out of each slice of toast.

Transfer to individual plates, garnish with watercress, Parmesan, and a drizzle of Lemon Dressing, and serve.

AFTERLIFE

About 1.3 billion tons of food is wasted every year with 85 percent of that waste going un-composted, resulting in 8 percent of the world's greenhouse gas emissions. AfterLife, founded by Sierra and Winson, is simplifying the process of upcycling food scraps from major urban markets; they haul the food waste from food establishments and turn the waste into fresh and delicious mushrooms. AfterLife also works with landlords and communities to help them comply with local laws, bolster sustainability efforts, and reuse food waste.

MORE ABOUT MUSHROOMS

Culinary mushrooms are a diverse group of fungi that are widely used in cooking for their unique flavors, textures, and nutritional benefits. Among the most common varieties are button mushrooms, shiitake, portobello, and oyster mushrooms.

Button mushrooms, also known as white mushrooms, are the most widely consumed. They have a mild flavor and are often used in salads, soups, and sautés. When left to mature, these mushrooms become portobellos, which have a dense texture and a rich, meaty flavor, making them a popular substitute for meat in vegetarian dishes.

Shiitake mushrooms are prized for their earthy, smoky taste and are commonly used in Asian cuisines. They are often found in soups, stir-fries, and as a flavoring in broths. Oyster mushrooms have a delicate texture and a slightly sweet flavor. They are versatile and can be grilled, sautéed, or added to soups.

Mushrooms are also valued for their health benefits, being low in calories and rich in vitamins, minerals, and antioxidants. They provide a good source of B vitamins, selenium, and potassium, and are known for their potential immune-boosting properties. Culinary mushrooms add depth and complexity to a wide range of dishes.

MEET OUR SOMMELIER

ANDRIJA TADEJEVIC

Andrija, who was born in Split, Croatia, in 1985, grew up surrounded by a rich winemaking tradition that has thrived for more than 2,500 years. This upbringing introduced him to the art of grape cultivation and the cultural significance of wine from an early age. For Andrija, it wasn't just about the wine itself, but the stories, traditions, and relationships that revolved around it. He witnessed firsthand how wine had the power to connect people, whether through shared meals, harvest festivals, or the simple act of toasting to health and happiness.

This environment sparked Andrija's curiosity about wine pairing and winemaking, leading him to pursue a degree in Viticulture and Enology at the College of Agriculture. The educational experience laid the foundation for his exciting career in the wine industry.

Andrija's professional journey began as a sommelier on Celebrity Cruises, where he honed his skills in wine selection and customer service. He later assumed the role of wine buyer for the Celebrity Cruise fleet, which further expanded his expertise in wine procurement and inventory management. His successful transition to this new role showcased his resilience and determination.

In 2015, Andrija moved to New York City, where he continued to thrive in the culinary scene. He began working as a sommelier at SD26, gaining valuable experience in a dynamic environment. Today, Andrija serves as our Wine Director at BLACKBARN Restaurant, a role that truly reflects his passion for wine. His knowledge and love for wine are evident in the impressive selection he curates, which perfectly complements our culinary offerings.

SPRING

What Spring doesn't deliver in an abundant bounty, this exciting season delivers in rejuvenation, especially in the Northeast where we get to enjoy all four seasons. By the time March rolls around, many of us are over winter. It's too late to ski and too early to put the coat and boots away, so we just wait and dream with anticipation for the first crocus and daffodils to bloom, the grass to turn green again, and the temperatures to climb enough to not have to wear a coat. In the kitchen, we get a slightly different sense of joy from spring with the anticipation of local rhubarb, green and white asparagus, ramps, fava beans, fiddlehead ferns, radishes, herbs, and a beautiful variety of mushrooms followed by fresh, crisp peas. Spring also delivers decadent lamb, soft-shelled crabs, and an abundance of freshwater bass, pike, salmon, and trout. Spring brings many opportunities to create memorable meals, and I'm pleased to share some of my favorites with you.

GARDEN

WHITE ASPARAGUS
WITH MOREL MUSHROOMS AND BUTTERMILK DRESSING

SERVES 4 TO 6

HOMEMADE VEGETABLE STOCK
MAKES 8 CUPS

2 quarts cold water
2 Spanish onions, peeled, charred, and roughly chopped
1 large carrot, roughly chopped
1 celery stalk, roughly chopped
5 cloves garlic, peeled and smashed
2 parsnips, roughly chopped
10 sprigs fresh thyme, roughly chopped
4 bay leaves

MOREL MUSHROOMS
MAKES 1½ CUPS

3 tablespoons olive oil
2 shallots, peeled and minced
3 thyme sprigs
½ pound morels, brushed and cleaned
⅛ cup sherry vinegar
Kosher salt and fresh cracked black pepper, to taste

My passion for white asparagus came in the early days of my career when I cooked in Michelin-starred restaurants in Holland, Belgium, and France where arguably the most prized white asparagus reside. The difference between white and green asparagus is the way they are grown. White asparagus never see sunlight so chlorophyl never develops, leaving them white and wonderfully sweet. Farmers will pile up soil as the asparagus grows and add a canvas cover to ensure no sunlight ever reaches them. The growing season is only from late April to early June, so we make sure we plan accordingly, and you should too when looking for them at your local market.

Begin by making the Homemade Vegetable Stock: Add the water to a 4-quart saucepot along with the onions, carrot, celery, garlic, parsnips, thyme, and bay leaves. Bring to a simmer and cook for 45 minutes, then strain the liquid through a fine mesh strainer into the desired container. Set aside until ready to use or refrigerate in an airtight container for up to 1 week.

To make the Morel Mushrooms: Add the oil to a 10-inch sauté pan over medium-high heat. When oil is heated and shimmering, add the shallots and thyme and sauté until the shallots are translucent, 2 to 3 minutes. Add the morels and continue to sauté until all their water has been released. Add the sherry vinegar and cook until nearly dry. Season to taste with salt and pepper, set aside, and let cool before using.

(Continued)

BUTTERMILK DRESSING
MAKES 3½ CUPS
2 cucumbers, grated
2 cups buttermilk
½ cup crème fraîche
½ cup mayonnaise
1 clove garlic, peeled and
    minced
¼ cup lime juice
1 lime, zested
1 teaspoon paprika
¼ cup apple cider vinegar
Kosher salt and fresh cracked
    black pepper, to taste

OTHER
4 cups whole milk
2 sticks unsalted butter
¼ cup lemon juice
⅛ cup sugar
½ piece vanilla bean, scraped
Kosher salt, to taste
15 stalks white asparagus,
    peeled and trimmed
1½ cups Morel Mushrooms
½ cup Buttermilk Dressing

To make the Buttermilk Dressing: In a mixing bowl, add the cucumber, buttermilk, crème fraîche, mayonnaise, garlic, lime juice, lime zest, paprika, and vinegar. Mix well with a wire whisk. Season with salt and pepper and refrigerate until ready to use.

Add the milk, butter, 2 cups of the Vegetable Stock, lemon juice, sugar, and vanilla bean to a 3-quart pot over low-medium heat. Stir to combine and season to taste with salt. Add the peeled asparagus and cook for 8 or 9 minutes or until al dente and the asparagus have a nice crunch. Readiness can be tested by piercing a stalk with a steak knife. If you prefer softer asparagus, cook for about 12 minutes. Remove the asparagus and let cool in the refrigerator.

Arrange the chilled asparagus on a serving platter. Place the Morel Mushrooms in a bowl and dress with the Buttermilk Dressing. Spoon the dressed morels over the asparagus and serve.

RICOTTA ZEPPOLE
WITH PRESERVED TOMATO AND WHITE BEAN PURÉE

SERVES 4 TO 6

PRESERVED TOMATOES
MAKES 3 CUPS

1 quart cherry tomatoes
1 cup sugar
1 tablespoon water
6 fresh basil leaves
Sea salt, to taste

WHITE BEAN PURÉE
MAKES 2¼ CUPS

2 (8-ounce) cans cannellini
    beans, drained
½ cup mascarpone cheese
¼ cup grated fresh Parmesan
    cheese
4 tablespoons extra virgin
    olive oil
1 teaspoon sea salt
⅛ teaspoon fresh cracked
    black pepper

BASIL PESTO
MAKES 1½ CUPS

2 cups packed fresh basil,
    freshly washed
2 to 3 cloves garlic, peeled
⅓ cup pine nuts (or walnuts)
½ cup grated fresh Parmesan
    cheese
½ cup extra virgin olive oil
Sea salt, to taste
Fresh cracked black pepper,
    to taste

RICOTTA ZEPPOLE

1½ cups all-purpose flour
4 large eggs
1½ teaspoons sugar
4 teaspoons baking powder

Growing up on Long Island, I had my share of summer carnivals and circuses where I would find funnel cake, cotton candy, zeppole, sausage, and peppers among some of the crowd favorites. My go-to was the zeppole. A dough made with ricotta cheese, fried crispy on the outside and soft on the inside, then tossed with sugar. Now as a chef, I tend not to leave anything alone, especially when it excites me. At BLACKBARN, my team and I get inspired to bring something like zeppole to the next level or completely transform it. We often ask ourselves: Why does it have to be sweet? Can we make it savory, and if so, what would we want to eat with it? And so, we did, and here it is.

To make the Preserved Tomatoes: Preheat the oven to 420°F. Line a baking sheet with parchment paper or aluminum foil. Spread the cherry tomatoes evenly across the sheet. Bake until the skins of the tomatoes blister, about 8 minutes.

Add the sugar and water to a 1-quart saucepan over medium heat. Mix with a rubber spatula until the mixture resembles wet sand. Bring to a simmer. Once simmering, remove from heat, then add the cooked tomatoes and any residual liquid. Bring the pot back to medium heat and allow to cook for 4 minutes. Remove the mixture from the heat and add the basil leaves and season with salt. Once cooled, store in an airtight container in the refrigerator for up to 2 weeks.

To make the White Bean Purée: Add the beans, cheeses, oil, salt and pepper to a food processor. Purée until smooth. With a rubber spatula, store the purée in a food-safe container in the refrigerator, for up to 4 days.

To make the Basil Pesto: Add the basil, garlic, pine nuts, cheese and oil to a blender and blend on high speed until smooth. Season with

(Continued)

2 cups ricotta cheese
¾ cup grated fresh Parmesan
  cheese, divided
1 teaspoon chopped fresh
  rosemary
1 teaspoon sea salt
4 cups coconut or avocado oil
  for frying

salt and pepper. The dressing will last in the refrigerator in an airtight container for up to 1 week.

To make the Ricotta Zeppole: Add the flour, eggs, sugar, baking powder, ricotta cheese, ½ cup Parmesan cheese, rosemary, and salt to a medium-sized mixing bowl. Mix well. Note: The dough will be sticky and tacky.

Add the frying oil to a 2-quart saucepan over medium-high heat. Bring the oil to 350°F. Use a candy or digital thermometer to gauge the temperature. When the oil reaches temperature, scoop the batter directly into the hot oil using a 2-ounce scoop. Note: Gently and carefully drop the dough ½-inch above the oil to prevent splashing. Allow to fry for 8 minutes, or until a toothpick inserted into the center of the Zeppole comes out clean.

Evenly distribute the Preserved Tomatoes, White Bean Purée, and Zeppole onto serving plates. Drizzle with ¼ cup of the Basil Pesto, sprinkle with the remaining Parmesan cheese, and serve.

🍷 Wine Suggestion
Dry Riesling, Finger Lakes, NY, USA

ROASTED HEIRLOOM CARROTS

WITH ENGLISH PEA HUMMUS

SERVES 4 TO 6

2 bunches fresh, heirloom baby carrots (about 12 carrots)
3 tablespoons olive oil
8 sprigs thyme, chopped
1 lemon, zested
2 cloves garlic, peeled and chopped
Kosher salt and fresh cracked black pepper, to taste

ENGLISH PEA HUMMUS
MAKES 5 CUPS

4 cups fresh English (sweet) peas
1 cup tahini paste
½ cup lime juice
1 lime, zested
2 tablespoons sesame oil
Kosher salt and fresh cracked black pepper, to taste

GARNISH

½ cup red seedless grapes, cut in half
4 cups watercress
2 tablespoons Lemon Dressing (page 108)
Papadum Chips, found at your local international food store, as needed, optional
Za'atar Spice (see Ingredient and Pantry), to taste, optional

We love our heirloom carrots. Whether we purchase them from the Union Square Market in town or from our farmer friend, Rick Bishop, owner of Mountain Sweet Berry Farms, we know they will be fresh, colorful, and flavorful no matter how we cook them. With this recipe, we'll be roasting the peas, in which the evaporation of water from inside the carrot leaves a concentration of flavor and caramelized sugars; something you will not achieve with boiling. For those who do boil or steam their carrots, these methods will create a clean flavor with beautiful and bright colors and a juicy mouthfeel. For those who like to eat their carrots raw, I suggest washing the carrots thoroughly but never peeling them as you will lose much of the nutrients found in the outer skin.

To make the Roasted Heirloom Carrots: Preheat the oven to 350°F. On a lined baking sheet, spread out the baby carrots. Drizzle them with the oil, followed by the thyme, lemon zest, and garlic. Season with salt and pepper. Toss the carrots together to coat them nicely. Place the baking sheet in the oven uncovered and roast for 18 minutes, or until the carrots are fork tender. Remove and allow to cool completely before serving.

To make the English Pea Hummus: Add the peas, tahini, lime juice, lime zest, and sesame oil to a food processor. Blend until a rough purée forms. Note: This recipe is meant to be chunky to add texture. Season to taste with salt and pepper.

Spread the hummus generously onto a serving platter. Place the roasted carrots on top. Garnish with grapes, watercress, a drizzle of Lemon Dressing, some Papadum Chips, a light dusting of Za'atar, and serve.

🍷 Wine Suggestion
Barbera d'Alba, Piedmont, Italy

WHAT ARE HEIRLOOM VEGETABLES?

Heirloom vegetables, like the carrots used in this recipe, are cherished for their rich flavors, historical significance, and genetic diversity. Unlike modern hybrids, which are bred for uniformity and shelf life, heirlooms are open-pollinated varieties passed down through generations. Each variety often has a unique story and a deep connection to a specific region or family. Their diverse shapes, colors, and tastes reflect the agricultural history and preferences of different cultures. Growing heirlooms can help preserve biodiversity and traditional farming practices. They also often thrive in organic and sustainable growing conditions, making them popular among gardeners and chefs who value authenticity and quality in their produce. By cultivating heirloom vegetables, we maintain a living link to our agricultural past and contribute to a more resilient food system.

OCEAN

CRAB CAKES
WITH SPINACH-RAMP PURÉE

SERVES 5 TO 7

CRAB CAKES
2 large eggs
¼ cup Dijon mustard
2 cups small-diced celery
1 tablespoon Old Bay
   Seasoning
Kosher salt to taste
Freshly cracked black pepper
   to taste
2 cups gluten-free panko
   breadcrumbs
½ cup mayonnaise
1 pound canned, lump crab
   meat, shells removed
4 tablespoons unsalted butter

SPINACH-RAMP PURÉE
1 gallon water for blanching
½ pound fresh baby spinach
15 fresh ramp tops, bulbs
   removed and reserved
2 tablespoons olive oil
2 medium shallots, peeled and
   small diced
5 tablespoons fresh lemon
   juice
¼ cup fresh mint leaves
Kosher salt and fresh cracked
   black pepper, to taste

Crab cakes are a beloved classic that evoke treasured memories of coastal summer getaways. These crisp golden bites are all about celebrating the delicate, sweet flavor of fresh crab meat. At BLACKBARN, we believe a true crab cake should let the crab shine, with just enough seasoning and binding to hold everything together. Whether enjoyed as an appetizer, an entrée, or tucked into a sandwich, crab cakes are a versatile dish perfect for a casual dinner or special occasion.

Prepare the Crab Cakes: Add the eggs, Dijon, celery, Old Bay, salt, pepper, panko, and mayonnaise to a medium bowl. Mix until fully incorporated. Gently fold in the crab meat, making sure to not crush the meat. Form into 5 to 7 crab cakes. Refrigerate until ready to cook.

To make the Spinach-Ramp Purée: Set a medium stockpot with 1 gallon of salted water over high heat. When boiling, add the spinach. Cook for 1 minute. Remove the spinach and immediately place in an ice bath. Add the ramp tops to the boiling water and cook for 2 minutes. Remove and immediately place in the ice bath with the spinach. Once cool, remove the spinach and ramp tops, squeeze out any excess water, and add to a blender and set aside. Add the olive oil to a medium sauté pan over high heat. When the oil is heated and shimmering, add the shallots and cook until translucent, about 2 minutes. Turn off the heat and add the lemon juice and mint leaves. Add the mixture to the blender with the spinach and ramp tops. Blend until smooth. Season with salt and pepper and set aside.

(Continued)

PICKLED RAMP BULBS

1 cup red wine vinegar
8 cups water
1 cup sugar
1 cinnamon stick
2 bay leaves
½ teaspoon peppercorns
½ teaspoon crushed red
   pepper flakes
1 star anise
15 reserved ramp bulbs (from
   the Spinach Ramp Puree)

OTHER

12 large asparagus, trimmed
   and peeled halfway down,
   cut 1½-inch
6 pods fava beans (about 30
   beans)
2 tablespoons unsalted butter
¼ cup shelled pistachio nuts
6 French breakfast radishes,
   sliced thin

To make the Pickled Ramp Bulbs: Add the vinegar, water, sugar, cinnamon stick, bay leaves, peppercorns, crushed red pepper, and star anise to a small pot over medium heat. Bring to a simmer then turn off the heat. Add the reserved ramp bulbs to a large mason jar. Strain the pickling liquid and pour over the ramp bulbs, making sure the bulbs are completely submerged. Place in the refrigerator until chilled, then cover until ready to use.

Place cleaned and peeled asparagus into salted boiling water for 2 minutes. Place in ice bath and set aside. Shell fava beans and add to salted boiling water for 3 minutes. Remove and place in ice bath with asparagus. Once cool, discard ice water and set asparagus and fava beans aside.

Preheat the oven to 350°F.

Heat 2 tablespoons of the butter in a 10-inch skillet over medium heat. Add the crab cakes and brown on both sides. Finish in the oven until they reach an internal temperature of 130°F. Keep warm.

Heat the Spinach-Ramp Puree in small pot. Warm the asparagus and fava beans in a small sauté pan over medium heat. Toast the pistachios in the preheated oven for 10 minutes, then finely chop.

To plate, spoon Spinach-Ramp Puree in center of each plate. Place one crab cake in the center of the puree. Mix asparagus, fava beans and pickled ramps in a small mixing bowl. Using a spoon, place on top of crab cake. Arrange the sliced radishes on top. Spoon the chopped pistachios on top of the crab cakes and serve.

🍷 Wine Suggestion
Pinot Noir Rose, Burgundy, France

PAN-SEARED DAY BOAT SCALLOPS

WITH CRISPY PANCETTA AND ENGLISH PEA RISOTTO

SERVES 4

CRISPY PANCETTA
4 (½-inch thick) slices pancetta

ENGLISH PEA PURÉE
MAKES 2 CUPS
1 tablespoon olive oil
½ shallot, diced
1 clove garlic, sliced
1 sprig thyme
1½ cups English peas, blanched
1 sprig mint, leaves picked
⅓ cup Homemade Vegetable Stock (page 172)
Kosher salt and white pepper to taste

ENGLISH PEA RISOTTO
SERVES 4 TO 6
8 tablespoons unsalted butter, divided
1 large Spanish onion, peeled and small diced
2 cups Carnaroli rice
1½ cups Pinot Grigio (or Chardonnay or Sauvignon Blanc)
7 cups Homemade Vegetable Stock (page 172)
1 cup English Pea Purée
1 cup freshly grated Parmesan cheese

SCALLOPS
2 tablespoons olive oil
12 (U10) dry-packed scallops, patted dry (see sizing; page 191)
2 tablespoons unsalted butter

Of all the fish we've ever put on the menu, nothing ever seems to be as popular as sea scallops. We receive the highest praise from our guests when we serve them, especially with a seasonal risotto that changes throughout the year, from fresh pea in the spring, to corn in the summer, and butternut squash in the fall and winter. Yes, I know what you're probably thinking up until now—that all our dishes seem to get the highest praise. It's important for me to make the designation because this is how our dishes become our signatures. For this recipe, I enjoy adding a little bacon, pancetta, or prosciutto as the saltiness really complements the sweetness of the scallops. When buying scallops, it's imperative to ask for "dry" scallops. That means they haven't been soaked in a solution to add weight, which will be drawn out when cooking, making them almost impossible to caramelize.

Begin by making the Crispy Pancetta: Preheat the oven to 350°F. Place the sliced pancetta on a lined baking sheet. Place in the oven for 18 minutes or until the fat has turned golden brown. Remove and place on a paper towel-lined plate to drain until ready to use.

To make the English Pea Purée: Add the olive oil to a 4-quart saucepot over medium-high heat. Once the oil is shimmering, add the shallot, garlic, and thyme. Allow to cook until the shallots turn translucent, stirring occasionally. Add the English peas, mint, and Vegetable Stock. Season with salt and pepper to desired taste and bring to a boil. Once boiling, remove from the heat. In a blender, puree all ingredients until smooth and transfer to the desired container until ready for use or refrigerate for up to 1 week.

To make the English Pea Risotto: Add 2 tablespoons of unsalted butter to a 4-quart saucepot over high heat. Melt the butter until foaming, then add the onions and sweat until translucent, about 3 to 4 minutes. Add the rice and toast, stirring consistently, for 5 minutes. Remove the

(Continued)

Kosher salt and fresh cracked black pepper, to taste

OTHER
4 to 6 pea tendrils, for garnish
Lemon Dressing (page 108), for garnish

pot from the heat and add the white wine. Return the pot to high heat and cook the wine until it has nearly evaporated, 4 to 6 minutes. While continuously stirring to release the starch, add ½ cup of Vegetable Stock. Cook the stock until nearly evaporated, about 3 minutes. Continue to add the stock in 3 to 4 stages, and stir until the rice is al dente, about 20 minutes. At this point, the starch should be released from the rice and be sticking to a wooden spoon. Reduce the heat to medium and fold in the English Pea Purée, remaining butter, and Parmesan cheese. Stir continuously until all the butter has melted and is incorporated evenly.

To make the Scallops: Add the olive oil to a 10-inch cast-iron skillet over high heat. When the oil is shimmering, season the scallops with salt and pepper and place them into the skillet with the flat surface down. Allow the scallops to sear untouched for 5 minutes, then flip the scallops and reduce the heat to medium. Add the butter and begin to baste the scallops with a spoon for another 4 minutes. Remove from the heat.

To serve: Divide the English Pea Risotto among 4 to 6 serving plates. Place the seared scallops on top, followed by the Crispy Pancetta, pea tendrils, and a drizzle of Lemon Dressing and serve.

Extra Wow Factor (Optional): After the scallops are seared and removed, add 1 clove garlic, 2 sprigs fresh thyme, and 2 black peppercorns. Cook until the garlic turns golden brown. Deglaze the pan with 4 tablespoons of white wine. Stir in the 4 tablespoons of cold butter and 1 tablespoon of Vegetable Stock. This sauce can now be spooned over the scallops for an added layer of deliciousness.

🍷 Wine Suggestion
Grenache Blanc, Rioja, Spain

MORE ABOUT DAY BOAT SCALLOPS

Harvested primarily along the Atlantic coast of the United States, particularly in New England, day boat scallops are larger and sweeter than bay scallops. They are typically harvested using dredges, though some fishermen use more sustainable methods like hand-harvesting by divers. This careful approach not only preserves the delicate marine environment but also results in scallops that are fresher and of higher quality than those caught by larger commercial fleets, which may spend days or weeks at sea before returning with their catch.

Day Boat scallops are "dry," meaning they haven't been treated with preservatives or chemicals, which is common with other scallops to retain water weight. This results in a pure, concentrated flavor and a better sear when cooked. They are a favorite among chefs and seafood enthusiasts, valued for their delicate, sweet taste and tender texture, making them a highlight in many fine dining dishes.

A NOTE ON SCALLOP SIZING

When purchasing scallops, sizing is an important factor to consider, as it can impact both the cooking process and the overall dining experience. Scallops are typically sized by the number per pound, with a lower number indicating larger scallops and a higher number indicating smaller ones.

U10: This size means there are fewer than 10 scallops per pound. These are the largest and most prized, often used in high-end dishes where presentation and texture are important.

10/20: This range indicates there are between 10 and 20 scallops per pound. These are medium to large scallops, commonly used in a variety of dishes, offering a balance between size and cost.

20/30: This size range means there are between 20 and 30 scallops per pound. These are smaller than the above sizes but still suitable for many recipes. They are often used in recipes where scallops are not the main focus.

30/40: This indicates there are between 30 and 40 scallops per pound. These are smaller and more affordable, suitable for dishes where the scallops are mixed with other ingredients.

When choosing scallops, consider the intended preparation and presentation. Larger scallops are ideal for searing and showcasing as the main ingredient, while smaller scallops work well in dishes like stews or pastas (i.e., sautéed with lemon butter or a hearty bouillabaisse).

PASTURE

BONE MARROW
WITH MANILA CLAMS AND SHALLOT REDUCTION

SERVES 4 TO 6

4 bone marrow pipes, split
lengthwise

BONE MARROW CRUST
MAKES 1¼ CUPS

1 cup panko bread crumbs,
divided
½ cup chopped fresh Italian
flat leaf parsley
¼ cup chopped fresh chives
¼ cup packed fresh basil leaves
1 tablespoon chopped fresh
thyme
¼ lemon, zested
1 clove garlic, peeled
2 tablespoons olive oil
Kosher salt, to taste

MANILA CLAMS

2 tablespoons olive oil
2 cloves garlic, peeled and
smashed
1 pound clams (or cockles),
soaked for 30 minutes in
cold water and strained
4 bay leaves
2 cups white wine (Chablis
or Chardonnay)

Here again, we have a classic dish with an added BLACKBARN twist. Traditionally, bone marrow is served on toast as its texture is quite soft and the crunchy toast creates the perfect balance. For us, we balance the soft marrow by adding Manila clams steamed in white wine, garlic, lemon and herbs, then topped with herb breadcrumbs. The clams add a pleasant chewy consistency, while the wine and lemon brighten the marrow with acidity and the crumbs provide the crunch. The combination is spectacular. This dish can be prepared ahead of time and finished in the oven when it's time to serve.

To prepare the bone marrow: Soak the bones in cold water for 12 to 24 hours, if desired.

Using a butter knife, gently scoop out the bone marrow, trying to keep the marrow as intact as possible. Once all bone marrow has been removed, cut the marrow into 1-inch pieces and set aside until ready to use.

To make the Bone Marrow Crust: Add ½ cup panko to a food processor along with the parsley, chives, basil, thyme, lemon zest, garlic, and olive oil. Blend until the mixture turns green. Add the remaining ½ cup panko and continue mixing until the mixture is green and appears slightly dry. Season with salt to taste and set aside until ready to use or store in an airtight container in the refrigerator for up to 1 week.

(Continued)

SHALLOT REDUCTION
1 tablespoon unsalted butter
1 shallot, peeled and minced
2 thyme sprigs
1 bay leaf
¼ cup white wine
¼ cup white wine vinegar
½ cup clam juice (from the
    Manila Clams recipe)
1 cup heavy cream
Sea salt and white pepper,
    to taste

To make the Manila Clams: Add the olive oil to a 3-quart saucepan with a lid over high heat. When the oil is heated and shimmering, add the garlic and toast until golden brown, 3 to 4 minutes. Add the clams, bay leaves, and wine. Cover and cook until the clams open. Once all the clams have opened, allow them to cool enough to handle. Pull out all clam meat from their shells and set the meat aside. Note: Discard any unopened clams. Using a fine mesh strainer, strain the cooking liquid to use in the Shallot Reduction recipe.

To make the Shallot Reduction: Add the butter to a 1-quart saucepot over medium heat. Melt the butter until it foams. Add the shallots, thyme, and bay leaf and let sweat until the shallots are translucent and have released their aroma, 2 to 3 minutes. Add the wine, vinegar, and clam juice. Reduce the liquid to ¼ cup and strain. Add the heavy cream and bring to a simmer. Reduce by half. Season to taste with salt and white pepper and set aside until ready to use, or store in an airtight container in the refrigerator for up to 2 weeks.

Preheat oven to 385°F.

Add the bone marrow, Shallot Reduction, and Manila Clams to 4 to 6 (5-inch in diameter) ramekins. Top with the Bone Marrow Crust and bake for 9 minutes. Remove from the oven and serve in the ramekins.

LAMB TWO WAYS
WITH STUFFED ZUCCHINI FLOWER

SERVES 4

LAMB RAGU
MAKES 1 CUP
1 tablespoon olive oil
1 clove garlic, peeled and
sliced
½ sprig fresh rosemary
¼ pound ground lamb
½ cup cherry tomatoes
1 cup chicken or vegetable
broth
2 tablespoons tomato purée
¼ cup medium-diced carrot

RACK OF LAMB
1 (2-pound, or 8-rib)
Frenched rack of lamb
Kosher salt and fresh cracked
black pepper, to taste
3 tablespoons olive oil
2 cloves garlic, peeled and
smashed
2 sprigs fresh rosemary
3 sprigs fresh thyme
6 tablespoons unsalted butter

STUFFED ZUCCHINI FLOWER
4 zucchini flowers
1 cup Lamb Ragu

From my experience, Colorado lamb is the standout winner when it comes to taste. I find the meat rich and buttery. As with any animal, there are both tender cuts and tough cuts. At BLACKBARN, we like to serve different cuts together in one dish. With this recipe, we've used ground shoulder, which we slowly braise, resulting in a sauce that pairs well with our roasted rack of lamb.

To make the Lamb Ragu: Add the olive oil to a 4-quart saucepot over medium-high heat. Heat until the oil is shimmering. Add the garlic and remove when golden brown, 4 to 5 minutes. Add the rosemary, followed by the ground lamb. Stir with a wooden spoon while breaking the lamb into smaller pieces. Return the toasted garlic along with the cherry tomatoes, broth, and tomato purée. Cook until the liquids start to boil. Reduce the heat to medium-low and simmer while adding the carrot. Continue cooking until the carrot pieces are fork-tender, 12 to 14 minutes. Remove from the heat and allow to cool. Use a spoon to evenly distribute the ground lamb into the 4 zucchini flowers.

To make the Rack of Lamb: Preheat the oven to 375°F. Season the lamb rack with salt and pepper. Add the olive oil to a 12-inch oven-safe skillet over high heat. When the oil is shimmering, add the seasoned lamb rack and sear the lamb chop for 4 minutes. Reduce the heat to medium-high and continue to sear until golden brown on all sides, 6 to 8 minutes. Add the garlic, rosemary, thyme, and butter. Reduce the heat to low and baste the lamb with the butter and herbs for 6 minutes. Place the pan into the oven and roast for about 9 minutes. Then, add the zucchini flowers to the pan with the partially cooked lamb and cook for another 5 minutes. The lamb should reach an internal temperature of 135°F when finished. Remove and let rest (the internal temperature will be 140°F to 145°F for medium). Slice the Lamb and serve immediately with the Stuffed Zucchini Flowers.

🍷 Wine Suggestion
Bordeaux Blend, Pomerol, France

IPA BRAISED CHESHIRE PORK SHANK

WITH CHARRED TOMATILLO RELISH

SERVES 4 TO 6

CHARRED TOMATILLO RELISH
MAKES 1 CUP

5 tomatillos
Kosher salt and fresh cracked
    black pepper, to taste
1 tablespoon olive oil
¾ cup Caramelized Onions
    (see below)
3 tablespoons Homemade
    Hot Sauce (page 92)

CARAMELIZED ONIONS
MAKES ¾ CUP

3 tablespoons olive oil
3 large white onions, peeled and
    sliced
2 bay leaves
4 sprigs thyme
Kosher salt and fresh cracked
    black pepper, to taste

PORK SHANK

4 tablespoons olive oil
4 Heritage "Cheshire" pork
    shanks, skinless
Kosher salt and fresh cracked
    black pepper, to taste
5 cloves garlic, peeled and
    smashed
2 large carrots, large diced
1 Spanish onion, peeled and
    large diced
6 sprigs fresh thyme
4 bay leaves
2 (12-ounce) bottles IPA beer
2 (12-ounce) bottles
    Belgian ale
2 (12-ounce) bottles
    stout beer
2 cups chicken broth

We love when meat just falls off the bone and you can eat it with a spoon. This braised pork shank is no exception. The more the animal's muscle is used, the tougher the meat but the more flavor it will have. We find braising is the best way to get a tough muscle tender without drying out the meat. We also believe using a variety of high-quality beers, which have sweet and tart notes, makes the best sauce for this dish. At the restaurant, we like to stand our pork shank up on the plate, creating a conversation piece. To do this, we cut the bottom of the shank with a bandsaw to create a flat surface. Ask your local butcher to do this for you if you'd like to mirror our presentation.

We're proud to use Niman Ranch pork for this dish. Niman Ranch is a network of over six hundred independent US family farmers and ranchers who raise their livestock humanely and sustainably. Their animals are raised outdoors or in deeply bedded pens, with no antibiotics, hormones, or crates—ever. This extra care results in a product that not only tastes better but consistently delivers a premium eating experience.

To make the Charred Tomatillo Relish: Preheat grill to 450°F. Remove the husks from the tomatillo and rinse the tomatillos well with water. Note: Using gloves will help keep the sap off your hands when handling. Add the tomatillos to a medium-sized mixing bowl. Add the oil and season with salt and pepper. Place the seasoned tomatillos on the grill and char on all sides. This will take 10 to 12 minutes while flipping and turning the tomatillos as they char. Once charred, remove them from the grill and set them aside to cool. Once cool, chop them into small pieces and add back to the bowl along with the Caramelized Onions and Hot Sauce. Mix well to combine. Set aside until ready to use or place in an airtight container and store in the refrigerator for up to 1 week.

(Continued)

BLACKBARN

To make the Caramelized Onions: Add the oil to a large sauté pan over medium high heat. Heat the olive oil until shimmering. Add half of the sliced onions, bay leaves, thyme, salt, and pepper. Allow the onions to sauté for 6 to 8 minutes untouched. Then, use a wooden spoon to scrape any sugars that are sticking to the bottom of the pan. Add the remaining onions and reduce the heat to low-medium. Continue cooking and scraping the sugars from the bottom of the pan, mixing the onions into the sugars that are caramelizing. After 15 to 20 minutes, the onions should look caramel-brown and are ready to be removed from the pan and used as needed.

To make the Pork Shanks: Prep the pork shank by removing any silver skin with a paring knife. Generously season all sides with salt and pepper and set aside.

Add the olive oil to a 6-quart stockpot over high heat. Heat the oil until it starts to shimmer. Once shimmering, lay the seasoned pork shanks on their sides in the pan. Sear all sides until golden brown. Note: Try not to move the shanks too much, as this will result in your pot getting cold and you will begin to "boil" instead of searing the meat. If there isn't enough room for all the shanks at once, sear in batches. Once the shanks are seared on all sides, remove them from the pot and set aside. Reduce the heat to medium-high and add the garlic, carrots, and onions. Cook untouched for 6 minutes, or until caramelization begins. Stir the vegetables with a wooden spoon and cook for another 6 minutes. Add the thyme and bay leaves and cook until aromatic, about 1 minute. Pour in the beers and chicken broth and set aside. Preheat the oven to 350°F.

Lay the Pork Shanks down in a roasting pan. Pour all of the beer mixture into the pan. Cover the pan with aluminum foil and cook in the oven for 2½ to 3 hours or until meat is fork tender (a fork can be inserted without resistance). When the meat is finished cooking, remove it from the roasting pan and set aside. Reduce the remaining liquid mixture on the stove over medium-high heat until it thickens slightly. Pour the sauce over the pork and top it with the Tomatillo Relish to serve.

🍷 Wine Suggestion
Shiraz, Barossa Valley, Australia

SIDES

SHISHITO PEPPERS

SERVES 4 TO 6

3 tablespoons olive oil
1½ pounds shishito peppers
1½ cups Pico De Gallo
   (page 220)
½ cup cotija cheese
Sea salt, to taste

Blistered shishito peppers, which is one of my go-to sides at BLACKBARN, is a simple yet flavorful dish, with the peppers quickly charred in a hot pan to bring out their smoky, mildly spicy flavor. Once blistered, we like to toss them with some of our homemade Pico de Gallo, which adds a zesty, tangy contrast with the tomatoes, onions, and cilantro. Before we serve the peppers, we'll quickly garnish with crumbled cotija cheese, lending a salty, creamy richness that complements the vibrant peppers.

Add the olive oil to a large cast-iron skillet over high heat. Heat the oil until shimmering. Add the shishito peppers and sauté, stirring often, for 4 minutes. Continue sautéing until the peppers start to blister. Once blistered and slightly charred, remove from the heat and add the Pico De Gallo. Give the pan a few tosses and spoon onto a serving platter. Garnish with the cheese, season with salt, and serve.

CRISPY ANNA POTATOES

SERVES 6 TO 8

10 Idaho (Russett) potatoes, peeled and thinly sliced lengthwise

4 sprigs fresh thyme, picked and chopped

1 sprig fresh rosemary, chopped

3 cloves garlic, peeled and chopped

2 sticks (16 tablespoons) unsalted butter, melted

4 tablespoons unsalted butter

Kosher salt and fresh cracked black pepper, to taste

These crispy potatoes, named after the famous Parisian courtesan Anna Deslions, who was known for her elegance and beauty, are another popular side at BLACKBARN. The potatoes are comforting and an elegant dish, perfect for any occasion. We thinly slice the potatoes, which are layered and infused with the earthy flavors of thyme and rosemary, along with garlic and butter. As the dish bakes, the potatoes absorb the rich flavors, become tender, and the top layer crisps up beautifully, offering a golden, crunchy contrast to the soft interior. The combination of the fresh herbs with the smooth potatoes creates a balanced and fragrant dish, making this satisfying side a hit night in and night out.

Preheat the oven to 360°F.

Add the sliced potatoes to a large bowl filled with cold water to prevent them from oxidizing.

Grease a 9 × 15-inch casserole dish until the bottom and sides of the pan are evenly covered. Add the potatoes in a shingled pattern. Each potato slice should overlap the last one. Once the first layer of potatoes is complete, sprinkle the thyme, rosemary, garlic, and salt evenly on top of the potatoes. Brush generously with the melted butter. Repeat the process until all the ingredients have been used.

Place in the oven and cook for 1 hour or until a knife can be inserted without resistance. Remove and, while still hot, use another similar pan or dish to press the potatoes into themselves and allow to cool for at least 4 hours or overnight in the refrigerator.

Preheat the oven to 425°F.

Turn the potatoes out onto a cutting board and cut into 2 × 2-inch squares. Bake for 25 to 30 minutes, or until golden brown, remove and serve.

DESSERT

CHOCOLATE SOUFFLÉ

**MAKES SIX 6-OUNCE
SOUFFLÉS**

1½ cups whole milk

¾ cup + 2 tablespoons sugar,
divided

½ piece vanilla bean, scraped

4 tablespoons unsalted butter,
softened, divided

3 tablespoons all-purpose
flour

1½ cups dark chocolate
(72% cacao)

½ cup egg yolks (from 6 to 8
large eggs)

1¼ cup egg whites (from 6 to
8 large eggs)

**Sometimes, I will revisit a recipe from my youth, and this is one of
them. When I was fifteen, I started cooking for a local restaurant
on Long Island. When my family realized that I could now cook,
they requested that I prepare a meal for them. I happily agreed. The
only problem was I wasn't trained in desserts. Reaching for the only
cookbook we had in the house at the time—a Time-Life cookbook
from the 50s—I turned to the page which featured the Chocolate
Soufflé. It was the most beautiful-looking dessert I had ever seen.
After successfully making it for my family, I later added the soufflé
to my menu at the Waldorf Astoria, and now here it is at BLACKBARN,
where it remains.**

Preheat the oven to 400°F.

Add the milk, 3 tablespoons sugar, and the pulp of the vanilla bean to a
small pot over medium heat and bring to a simmer.

Add 3 tablespoons of the butter and all of the flour to a mixing bowl.
Mix to combine. Pour the warm milk mixture into the butter and flour
mixture. Whisk well, pour back into the pot over medium heat, and
cook until thickened, about 6 minutes. Pour into a large mixing bowl
and set aside to cool.

Melt the chocolate in a double broiler, mixing with a rubber spatula or
wooden spoon until fully melted. Set the chocolate aside.

(Continued)

Once the thickened milk base has cooled, mix in the egg yolks and melted chocolate until fully incorporated.

In a separate bowl, whisk together the egg whites and 9 tablespoons of sugar until stiff peaks form. Gently fold a third of the meringue into the chocolate mixture with a rubber spatula. Repeat twice or until all the meringue has been incorporated. To avoid overmixing, stop folding when the batter has a marbled look, just before it has totally blended.

Use the remaining tablespoon of butter to coat the interior of six 6-ounce soufflé dishes. Use the remaining 2 tablespoons of sugar to coat the buttered dishes. Pour the mixture into the dishes and bake for 20 to 25 minutes. Remove and let cool slightly before serving.

ROASTED FIGS AND ALMOND SHORTBREAD

WITH WHIPPED RICOTTA

SERVES 4

ALMOND SHORTBREAD
SERVES 4

2 cups unsalted butter, diced
¼ teaspoon kosher salt
1 cup sugar
3 large eggs
1 vanilla bean, scraped
2½ tablespoons almond
   extract
3 cups all-purpose flour

WHIPPED RICOTTA
MAKES 2¼ CUPS

½ cup softened goat cheese
¼ cup Vermont maple syrup
1 cup whole milk ricotta
4 tablespoons olive oil
Sea salt, to taste

OTHER

8 Black Mission figs (or any
   other fresh figs), cut in half
¼ cup turbinado cane sugar
   (Sugar in the Raw™)
2 tablespoons apple balsamic
   vinegar

We love figs at BLACKBARN. We put them on pizza and make fig jam to go with our cheese board, and on a ham and brie baguette. When it comes to dessert, we roast the figs just long enough to release their juices and then enjoy them with whipped ricotta and goat cheese on a buttery, almond sablé. It's as good as it gets.

Begin by making the Almond Shortbread: Preheat the oven to 375°F. Add the butter, salt, and sugar to a stand mixer with the paddle attachment. Mix until the mixture is creamy, light, and fluffy, about 4 minutes. Add the eggs one at a time, waiting until the last egg is completely incorporated before adding the next egg. Add the vanilla and almond extract. Continue mixing on low speed. Add the flour and mix until a homogenous dough forms. Do not overmix as this will result in a tougher, harder shortbread. Remove the dough from the bowl and transfer to a lightly floured surface. Roll the dough to ⅛-inch thickness. Cut into 2 × 4-inch rectangles. Place on a parchment-lined baking sheet and bake for 9 to 12 minutes, or until lightly golden brown. Remove and set aside.

To make the Whipped Ricotta: Add the goat cheese, syrup, ricotta, and olive oil to a mixing bowl. Mix until incorporated. Season with salt and set aside.

Preheat a broiler. Prepare the figs by sprinkling the sugar on top of the cut side of the figs and arranging them on a sheet pan. Place the figs under the broiler for 4 to 7 minutes, or until the sugars are caramelized. Set aside.

Place the Almond Shortbread onto the desired plates. Spoon the Whipped Ricotta on top of the shortbreads. Arrange the figs on top of the Whipped Ricotta, drizzle the vinegar over the top, and serve.

SUMMER

For me, summertime is one of the most enjoyable times of the year. The beach, the lake, the pool . . . the garden! For those who don't have a garden, the local farmers' markets have plenty of ripe tomatoes, sweet corn, fragrant peaches, and melon, as well as lettuces, green beans, and cucumbers for salads, and don't forget the fresh basil for homemade pesto. Summer also means vacations and long weekends; outdoors more than indoors; campfires under the stars. And let's not forget the bounty of the sea, which involves oysters and champagne, mussels and beer, lobster rolls, and fried clams. Then there's the barbecues, cookouts, and relaxing summer days smoking meats. When I grill at home, I'll use lump charcoal and wood chunks to get a delicious smoky flavor into the meat. When grilling, it's important to start with a high flame/temperature to allow the meat to caramelize before reducing the flame or shifting the meat to a cooler part of the grill to finish the interior to the desired temperature.

GARDEN

GRILLED CORN AND KALE SALAD

WITH PICKLED JALAPEÑOS

SERVES 4 TO 6

PICKLED JALAPEÑOS
MAKES ABOUT 2 CUPS

1 cup white wine vinegar

1 cup water

⅓ cup sugar

1 tablespoon kosher salt

1 sprig fresh thyme

1 bay leaf

10 jalapeños, sliced

¼ cup carrot, diced

¼ cup Spanish onion, diced

BACON LARDONS
MAKES 1 CUP

½ pound bacon slab, cut into ¼-inch thick and 1-inch-long pieces (lardons)

OTHER

4 ears bicolor corn, grilled, corn removed from cob

1½ pounds green kale, chopped

3 cups halved cherry tomatoes

½ cup Pickled Jalapeños

1 cup Bacon Lardons

1 head radicchio, chopped

2 avocados, diced

2½ cups Green Goddess Dressing (page 112)

¼ pound Ricotta Salata

Kosher salt and fresh cracked black pepper, to taste

We like to have kale salad on our menu, however, the garnishes change seasonally. As many of our guests look for healthy options, we've managed to make it the most enjoyable by cutting it finer than usual. We've also added a healthy amount of roasted seasonal vegetables and a grain to enrich the texture. And we've spiced up the dressing and added pickled jalapeños. For a vegan option, simply substitute the Avocado Green Goddess Dressing with 1 cup Lemon Dressing (page 108).

To make the Pickled Jalapeños: Add the vinegar, water, sugar, and salt to a 2-quart saucepot over high heat. Bring to a boil, then add the thyme, bay leaf, jalapeños, onion, and carrot. Reduce the heat to medium-low and simmer for 10 minutes. Remove the saucepot from the heat and allow to cool completely. Once cooled, discard the thyme and bay leaf. Slice the jalapenos in half and seed 5 of them. Add them to a large mason jar. Add the carrot and onion to the jar. Completely cover with the vinegar mixture, seal, and refrigerate until ready to use, for up to 2 to 4 months.

To make the Bacon Lardons: Add the lardons to a large cast iron skillet over medium heat and cook untouched for 8 minutes. Use a spoon to flip and move the lardons around, allowing the remaining sides to render their fat. Continue gently moving the lardons until crispy. Strain the grease and transfer the lardons to a paper towel. Set aside until ready to serve.

(Continued)

To assemble the salad: Add the corn, kale, tomatoes, Pickled Jalapeños, Bacon Lardons, radicchio, avocado, and the Green Goddess Dressing to a large bowl. Toss until combined. Plate and grate the desired amount of Ricotta Salata on top, season with salt and pepper and serve.

🍷 Wine Suggestion
Albarinho, Galicia, Spain

WATERMELON SALAD
WITH BLUE CHEESE DRESSING AND BERMUDA ONIONS

SERVES 4 TO 6

BLUE CHEESE DRESSING
MAKES 2½ CUPS
1 cup blue cheese
¼ cup white wine vinegar
6 to 8 tablespoons water
4 tablespoons olive oil
Kosher salt, to taste
White pepper, to taste

MIXED HERB SALAD
MAKES 1 CUP
8 leaves fresh Italian flat leaf
  parsley
4 leaves fresh mint
4 sprigs fresh dill, stems
  removed
8 chives, cut into ½-inch sticks

BERMUDA ONIONS
1 Bermuda onion, peeled and
  thinly sliced
½ cup kosher salt

OTHER
1 watermelon, rind and seeds
  removed; flesh cut into
  wedges

Can we really say summer without mentioning the word watermelon? The smell and taste of fresh, local watermelon says summer like no other fruit . . . okay, maybe the peach. Every summer at BLACKBARN, we'll serve a variation of watermelon salad, especially during the lunch rush. Sometimes we'll compress the watermelon with rosemary-infused olive oil, or as featured in this recipe, keep the melon fresh, allowing its natural fragrant and mouthwatering sweetness to stand out while elevating the dish with a slight garnish of homemade Blue Cheese Dressing, fresh herbs, and sliced Bermuda onions.

To make the Blue Cheese Dressing: Add the blue cheese and vinegar to a medium-sized bowl. Gradually add 6 to 8 tablespoons water until a thick dressing-like consistency is reached. Stir in the olive oil, season with salt and pepper, and serve. The dressing can be stored in an airtight container in the refrigerator for up to 1 week.

To make the Mixed Herb Salad: Add the parsley, mint, dill, and chives to a small bowl. Toss and refrigerate until ready to use. This salad should be used as soon as possible to ensure freshness.

To make the Bermuda Onions: Add the onions to a bowl filled with 4 cups water, 2 cups ice, and the salt. Let the onions soak for 10 minutes.

To plate, arrange the watermelon wedges onto individual serving plates. Drizzle the Blue Cheese Dressing over the watermelon, Sprinkle the Bermuda Onions around the plate followed by the Mixed Herbs, and serve.

Wine Suggestion
Sweet Chenin Blanc, Vouvray, France

OCEAN

BIGEYE TUNA TARTARE

SERVES 4 TO 6

TUNA TARTARE
12 ounces fresh bigeye tuna
3 tablespoons thinly sliced
    chives
1 medium lemon, zested
2½ tablespoons Lemon
    Dressing (page 108)
1 tablespoon sea salt

GUACAMOLE
MAKES 2 CUPS
2 ripe avocados, medium diced
¼ cup peeled and diced red
    onion
1 tablespoon chopped fresh
    cilantro
1 lime, juiced
1½ tablespoons deseeded and
    diced jalapeño
½ tablespoon sea salt
¼ teaspoon fresh cracked
    black pepper

PICO DE GALLO
MAKES 1½ CUPS
1 cup small-diced vine-
    ripened tomatoes
½ cup peeled and small-diced
    red onion
1 jalapeño, deseeded and diced

Tuna Tartare is another one of the most popular items on our menu. Whether enjoyed as a casual bar snack in our Tavern, as a shared appetizer in our more refined Main Dining Room, or as part of our exquisite family-style event dinners, this dish never fails to impress. The key to its deliciousness is the quality and freshness of the tuna itself. This recipe is an excellent example of how we impart a contrast of textures into each dish. The bright acidity of the Pico de Gallo complements the soft, creamy tuna and avocado while the crispy, fried tortilla strips offer the perfect finishing touch with a satisfying crunch.

Place the tuna on a clean, non-porous cutting board and dice into small cubes. Add the tuna to a medium-sized mixing bowl along with the chives, lemon zest, Lemon Dressing, and sea salt. Mix well, cover, and refrigerate until ready to serve.

To make the Guacamole: Add the avocado, onion, cilantro, lime juice, and jalapeño to a medium bowl. Mix well. Season with salt and pepper. Refrigerate until ready to serve.

To make the Pico de Gallo: Add the tomatoes, onion, jalapeño, cilantro, lime juice, salt, and pepper to a medium mixing bowl and mix until combined. Refrigerate in a sealed container for at least 10 minutes until ready to serve.

To make the Tortilla Strips: Add the frying oil to a 2-quart saucepan over medium-high heat. Bring the oil to 350°F. Use a candy or digital

(Continued)

1½ tablespoons (loosely packed) chopped fresh cilantro
3 tablespoons fresh lime juice
1 teaspoon sea salt
¼ teaspoon fresh cracked black pepper

TORTILLA STRIPS
MAKES 2½ CUPS
2 (6-inch) white corn tortillas, julienned
4 cups coconut or avocado oil for frying
½ tablespoon kosher salt

thermometer to gauge the temperature. While the oil is reaching temperature, line a sheet tray with paper towels. When oil reaches temperature, reduce the heat to medium-low. Add the julienned tortillas and fry until golden brown, 3 to 4 minutes. Use a spider or slotted spoon to remove the tortilla strips from the oil. Let as much oil as possible run off the tortilla strips before transferring to the pre-lined sheet tray. Once all the strips are on the tray, season with salt and set aside until ready to use.

Select the appropriate-sized serving plate or platter for either individual or family-style dining. Place a ring mold directly onto each plate. Divide the tuna mixture equally inside the ring molds, gently packing it down with a spoon. Divide the Guacamole on top of each tuna portion and carefully remove the ring molds. Garnish with the Pico de Gallo and Tortilla Strips and serve.

BUTTER POACHED MAINE LOBSTER

WITH FRESH PEA SOUP

SERVES 4

FRESH PEA SOUP
MAKES 3 CUPS

3 tablespoons olive oil
1 medium shallot, peeled and
　　sliced
1 clove garlic, peeled and
　　sliced
3 fresh thyme springs, tied
　　into a bouquet
1 bay leaf
1½ cups white wine
6 cups English peas, blanched
12 mint leaves
Kosher salt and white pepper,
　　to taste

LOBSTER

2 (1½ pound) live Maine
　　lobsters
1½ cups heavy cream
1 stick (8 tablespoons)
　　unsalted butter, diced
½ vanilla bean, scraped
Kosher salt and white pepper,
　　to taste

Nothing says summer on the east coast like lobster. This recipe and cooking method brings out the finest qualities that lobster has to offer. Adding cream to the butter adds an extra degree of richness, while the vanilla intensifies the natural sweetness of the lobster. In this recipe, we've paired our fresh-cooked lobster with a sweet pea soup which brings out the lobster's natural sweetness. The addition of mint in the soup provides a refreshing contrast, while the creamy, rich texture of the soup mirrors the richness of the butter-poached lobster, allowing both elements to shine without overpowering one another.

To make the Fresh Pea Soup: Add the olive oil to 2-quart saucepot. Heat until the oil is shimmering. Add the shallot and garlic and cook until translucent, about 4 minutes. Add the thyme and bay leaf and cook for 2 minutes. Add the white wine and bring to a boil. Once boiling, add the blanched English peas and mint. Remove from the heat. Blend the soup in a blender until smooth. Season with salt and pepper and set aside.

To make the Lobster: Bring a salted pot of water to a boil over high heat. Once boiling, add the lobsters and cook for 3 to 4 minutes. Remove and immediately transfer to an ice bath then remove the meat from the tail and claws and set aside. Add the heavy cream to a 2-quart saucepot over medium-high heat. Bring to a low boil. Once boiling, add the butter and vanilla. Using a whisk, stir until the butter is well incorporated. Season with salt and pepper. Add the lobster and allow to cook for 2 to 3 minutes. Note: The lobster meat can be chopped or left whole. Add the Fresh Pea Soup to 4 shallow bowls. Arrange the lobster meat in the middle. Drizzle a spoonful of vanilla sauce around the soup and serve.

🍷 Wine Suggestion
Blanc de Blanc - Chardonnay Champagne, France

ROASTED BRANZINO
WITH SPICED ROASTED CARROTS AND PAN ROASTED POTATOES

SERVES 4 TO 6

HERB MIX
MAKES 1½ CUPS
10 sprigs fresh Italian flat leaf
   parsley, chopped
4 sprigs fresh thyme, chopped
2 sprigs fresh rosemary,
   chopped
2 sprigs fresh tarragon,
   chopped
2 cloves garlic, peeled and
   chopped
½ tablespoon red chili flakes
1 orange, zested
1 cup olive oil

MARINATED OLIVES
2 cups Castelvetrano or green
   olives, pitted
1 orange peel
2 cloves garlic, peeled and
   smashed
½ fennel bulb, shaved
2 star anise
1 teaspoon red pepper chili
   flakes
6 tablespoons olive oil
1 tablespoon sea salt

SPICED ROASTED CARROTS
8 baby bunched carrots,
   cleaned and scrubbed
2 sprigs thyme, picked
2 cloves garlic, peeled and
   chopped
1 teaspoon ground coriander
Kosher salt and fresh cracked
   black pepper, to taste

I frequently hear from guests our Branzino is the best they've ever had, which just delights me and makes me happy to share it with you. I feel what makes our Branzino so delicious is the herb mixture which, by the way, will work well with pretty much any white flaky fish. This fish can be cooked in the oven if a grill isn't available and if you can throw some wood chips on the grill, the flavor will be elevated even further. When purchasing branzino, ask your local butcher or fishmonger to butterfly and debone the fish for you.

To make the Herb Mix: Add the parsley, thyme, rosemary, tarragon, garlic, chili flakes, orange zest, and olive oil to a medium-sized mixing bowl. Mix with a rubber spatula until well combined. Set aside until ready to use or place in an airtight container and refrigerate for up to 1 week.

To make the Marinated Olives: Add the olives, orange peel, garlic, fennel, star anise, chili flakes, olive oil, and salt to a medium-sized bowl. Mix well to combine. Allow the mixture to marinate at room temperature for at least 2 hours. Serve immediately or place into an airtight container in the refrigerator for up to 2 weeks.

To make the Spiced Roasted Carrots: Preheat the oven to 365°F. Add the carrots, thyme, garlic, coriander to a medium-sized bowl. Toss together until the carrots are coated and season with salt and pepper. Transfer the carrots to a lined baking sheet. Place on the middle rack of the oven and roast for 18 minutes. Remove and set aside until ready to serve.

To make the Pan Roasted Potatoes: Add the potatoes, garlic, and mint to a 4-quart saucepot set over high heat. Fill with cold water to just cover the top of the potatoes. Note: The more water in the pot, the less flavor the potatoes will have. Bring to a boil then reduce the heat to a simmer. Cook for 15 minutes, or until potatoes are fork tender. Strain the potatoes and let cool for 15 minutes. Place the cooled potatoes on

(Continued)

PAN ROASTED POTATOES

1 pound butterball or Yukon
  potatoes
5 cloves garlic, peeled and
  smashed
4 sprigs fresh mint
¼ cup unsalted butter
¼ cup olive oil
Kosher salt to taste

GRILLED LEMON

2 large lemons
1 tablespoon olive oil
Kosher salt to taste

BRANZINO

2 (2½ pound) Branzinos,
  butterflied and deboned
Sea salt and fresh cracked
  black pepper, to taste

a cutting board and press them one by one with your hand. They should be flat but not broken. Add the butter and oil to a cast iron skillet over medium-high heat. Melt the butter until it foams. Add the potatoes until the bottom of the skillet is covered (the potatoes can be touching but not on top of one another). Continue cooking the potatoes untouched for 8 minutes. Flip the potatoes over and repeat until all the potatoes are crispy. Season with salt and transfer to a paper towel-lined plate to drain. Set aside until ready to use.

To make the Grilled Lemon: Preheat an outdoor grill to medium-high heat. Cut the lemons in half. Drizzle with olive oil on the open side of each half, season with salt, and grill until charred. Alternatively, caramelize in a cast iron skillet. Set aside.

To make the Branzino: Preheat the oven to 385°F. Rinse the branzino under cold running water and pat dry. Check and remove any pin bones that remain with kitchen tweezers. To remove the bones, gently run your finger along the bloodline or centerline of each filet. You will feel the pin bones, which are located starting from the collar to the middle of the filet. Place the branzino on a lined baking sheet and open the fish with the flesh side facing up. Season with salt and pepper then abundantly rub the flesh with the Herb Mix. Close the fish and season both sides of the skin with salt and pepper. Place in the middle rack of the oven and roast uncovered for 18 minutes. Remove from the oven. While still hot, and using a spatula, gently move the fish onto a serving plate, keeping the fish as intact as possible. If the fish is sticking, gently try to release the fish by sliding a spatula under the fish in sections until it's free.

Arrange the fish on a platter. Squeeze the Grilled Lemon over the Branzino, garnish with the Marinated Olives, Spiced Roasted Carrots, and Pan Roasted Potatoes and serve.

🍷 Wine Suggestion
Roussanne, Marsanne - Chateauneuf du Pape, France

POLENTA CAKE
WITH RATATOUILLE AND MARINATED SHRIMP

SERVES 4 TO 6

RATATOUILLE
MAKES 3 CUPS

2 tablespoons olive oil (plus 1 additional tablespoon if reheating)
1 cup diced red onion
Sea salt, to taste
1 cup diced red bell pepper
1 cup diced zucchini
1 cup diced vine-ripe tomatoes
4 cloves garlic, peeled and chopped
1½ tablespoons aged sherry vinegar
⅛ teaspoon chili flakes
2 basil chiffonade leaves
2 tablespoons tomato purée
⅛ teaspoon fresh cracked black pepper

MARINATED SHRIMP

1 pound (16/20) raw shrimp, peeled and deveined
2 cloves garlic, peeled and chopped
1 tablespoon grated lemon zest
4 sprigs fresh thyme
4 tablespoons olive oil, divided
⅛ teaspoon fresh cracked black pepper
1 teaspoon sea salt

POLENTA CAKE
MAKES 7 CUPS

2 cups whole milk
2 cups water
1 tablespoon sea salt

This is a relatively new dish at BLACKBARN, but a wonderful addition to the many favorites our guests have come to enjoy over the years. The creamy-cheesy polenta makes the perfect match to our brightly flavored Ratatouille and slightly charred shrimp. There are multiple variations one can make with this dish. The polenta can be made without cheese and served soft, right from the pot. Seared sea scallops or chicken will also work well if you prefer another protein besides shrimp.

To make the Ratatouille: Add the olive oil to a large sauté pan over medium-high heat. When the olive oil starts to shimmer, add the red onion, season with salt, and cook for 2 minutes. Add the bell pepper, season with salt, and cook for 2 minutes. Repeat the process with the zucchini, tomatoes, and garlic. Add the sherry, chili flakes, basil, tomato purée, and season with pepper. Toss until well combined. Remove from the heat and set aside. If not using immediately, chill right away in the refrigerator to preserve the vegetables' bright colors. To reheat before serving: Add 1 tablespoon of olive oil to a large sauté pan over medium-low heat. When the oil is heated, add the ratatouille and cook, stirring occasionally, until warm, 5 to 8 minutes.

To make the Marinated Shrimp: Add the shrimp, garlic, lemon zest, thyme, 3 tablespoons of olive oil, salt, and pepper to a medium-sized bowl. Gently toss and allow to marinate in the refrigerator for a minimum of 5 minutes, up to 40 minutes.

To make the Polenta Cake: Add the milk, water, and salt to a 3-quart, stainless steel, lidded saucepan on high heat. Bring to a boil. Once boiling, add the polenta and use a wooden spoon to stir in a figure 8 motion. When the mixture slightly thickens, reduce the heat to low. Allow the polenta to cook for 35 minutes, checking every 10 minutes and stirring with a wooden spoon. When 35 minutes lapse, add the butter and cheese. Mix with a wooden spoon until the butter has

(Continued)

1 cup polenta
⅔ stick of unsalted butter, diced
½ cup grated fresh Parmesan cheese
1 tablespoon olive oil

melted and combined with the polenta. Pour the polenta into a pan (12¾" × 10⅜" with at least 1¼" depth) and place in the refrigerator for 30 to 40 minutes, or until chilled. Turn the polenta onto a cutting board and slice into the desired shape(s).

To finish the Shrimp: Add the remaining tablespoon of olive oil to a large sauté pan over high heat. When the olive oil starts to shimmer, add the marinated shrimp and sauté for 8 minutes. Remove from the heat and set aside.

To finish the Polenta Cake: Add the olive oil to a medium sauté pan over medium-high heat. When the olive oil starts to shimmer, add the polenta cake and allow to sear untouched for approximately 4 minutes. Flip the polenta over and repeat. Once seared on both sides, remove and arrange on individual plates. Top with the Ratatouille and Marinated Shrimp and serve.

🍷 Wine Suggestion
Pinot Gris, Alsace, France

A LITTLE RATATOUILLE HISTORY

Ratatouille is a traditional French dish that has its origins in the Provence region. Its name comes from the Provençal French word "ratatouille," which means "to stir up." The dish is a rustic vegetable stew featuring ingredients like eggplant, zucchini, bell peppers, tomatoes, onions, and herbs, all simmered together to create a harmonious blend of flavors.

Historically, ratatouille was a peasant dish, developed from the abundance of summer vegetables in the region. It was a practical and economical way to utilize seasonal produce. The earliest recorded versions of ratatouille date back to the eighteenth century, but the dish gained prominence in the nineteenth century.

The modern version of ratatouille, as we know it today, was popularized in the twentieth century, especially by renowned chefs who embraced its simplicity and the rich flavors of Provençal cuisine. It was further showcased globally by the 2007 Pixar film of the same name, which introduced the dish to a wider audience and celebrated its cultural significance.

PASTURE

GRILLED AMISH CHICKEN
WITH CHIMICHURRI AND PANZANELLA SALAD

SERVES 4 TO 6

AMISH CHICKEN
2 (2½-pound) Amish chickens,
    deboned
Kosher salt
10 to 12 sprigs fresh thyme
2 lemons, zested
6 cloves garlic, peeled and
    smashed

CHIMICHURRI
MAKES 3½ CUPS
3 sprigs fresh Italian flat leaf
    parsley, chopped
2 sprigs fresh mint, chopped
2 sprigs fresh dill, chopped
1 sprig fresh oregano,
    chopped
1 sprig fresh tarragon,
    chopped
6 chives, chopped
2½ cups olive oil
¼ cup red wine vinegar
Kosher salt and fresh cracked
    black pepper, to taste

TOMATO VINAIGRETTE
MAKES 1 CUP
3 tablespoons tomato purée
1 tablespoon tomato juice
⅛ cup Moscatel Vinegar (see
    Ingredients and Pantry)

Whenever guests ask me what they should order, I often recommend the chicken. That's because we've got it figured out. All too often chicken is under-seasoned, the meat is overcooked, and the skin is undercooked. By marinating the chicken overnight, the garlic, lemon, and thyme helps penetrate the flesh while salting the skin removes moisture, helping to make the chicken crispy in the pan or grill. By slowly cooking the chicken skin side down, the fat renders out making the skin crisp without overcooking the meat itself. In this recipe, patience is the main ingredient.

On a lined baking sheet, lay the chickens flat. Season both sides with the thyme, lemon zest, and garlic. Arrange skin side up and sprinkle with salt. Wrap the baking sheet with plastic wrap and place into the refrigerator. Allow to marinate for at least 3 hours, up to 24 hours.

To make the Chimichurri: Add the parsley, mint, dill, oregano, tarragon, and chives to a small bowl. Whisk in the oil and vinegar and season with salt and pepper. Set aside until ready to use, or store in an airtight container in the refrigerator up to 3 days.

To make the Tomato Vinaigrette: Add the tomato purée, tomato juice, both vinegars, and oregano to a small bowl. Whisk in the olive oil and season with salt. Set aside until ready to toss in the Panzanella Salad (using about ½ cup), or store in an airtight container in the refrigerator up to 2 weeks.

1 tablespoon sherry vinegar
1 sprig fresh oregano
¾ cup olive oil
Kosher salt, to taste

PANZANELLA SALAD
4 large heirloom tomatoes
2 cups heirloom cherry
    tomatoes
3 Persian cucumbers, sliced
1 red onion, peeled and thinly
    sliced
4 cups sourdough croutons

To make the Panzanella Salad: Add both kinds of tomatoes along with the cucumber, onion, and croutons in a large bowl. Mix well and set aside until ready to serve.

Preheat an outdoor grill to low heat.

Remove the chickens from the refrigerator and place onto the preheated grill, skin side down. Cook until the skin has browned. Turn the chicken to the flesh side and cook until the chickens reach an internal temperature of 165°F. Place the chickens on the desired plates or platter. Garnish with the Chimichurri, add the dressed Panzanella Salad off to the side and serve.

🍷 Wine Suggestion
Pinot Noir, Mosel, Germany

BLACKBARN TOMAHAWK
WITH HERB BUTTER

SERVES 4 TO 6

HERB BUTTER
MAKES 1½ CUPS
½ pound softened unsalted
    butter
6 sprigs chopped fresh thyme
3 sprigs chopped fresh
    rosemary
4 sprigs chopped fresh sage
6 sprigs chopped fresh Italian
    flat leaf parsley
Sea salt, to taste

TOMAHAWK STEAK
16 Roasted Garlic Cloves
    (page 316)
¾ cup Chipotle-Orange Spice
    Rub (page 134)
2 (30- to 36-ounce) large
    bone CAB tomahawk
    steaks
Sea salt, to taste

If steak were king, the tomahawk would be emperor. I am a dedicated Certified Angus Beef (CAB) user. That's because I've learned if a cow is stamped "CAB" by a USDA inspector, it means the beef passed ten high-quality standards to get that stamp. The stamp also signifies the flavor, texture, and mouthfeel of that burger or steak made with CAB coming off that ranch. Black-hided Angus cattle are naturally bred and built for larger muscles with plenty of marbling (the interior veins of fat within the muscle that deliver all the flavor). You may see a lot of "grassfed" marketing efforts behind lesser quality cattle, but know this: all cattle are grassfed, even if they are finished on a grain diet before they go to market. A cow that's only grassfed takes longer to develop, which often yields an older animal and likely a tougher steak. At BLACKBARN, we start with the best CAB tomahawk, add our own spice blend, grill the meat over wood, and present the decadent slab tableside on a hook with the beef bathed in garlic, rosemary, olive oil, and butter. It's simply mouthwatering.

To make the Herb Butter: Add the butter, thyme, rosemary, sage, and parsley to a medium mixing bowl. Mix well and season with sea salt. Use immediately or store in an airtight container in the refrigerator for up to 1 month.

Preheat an outdoor grill to 450°F.

Add the Roasted Garlic Cloves to a medium bowl and smash the cloves into a smooth paste. Add the Chipotle-Orange Spice Rub and mix well. Rub the paste onto the steaks, making sure to cover all sides. Season with salt and place onto the grill.

Leave the steaks on the grill untouched for 8 minutes. Note: If the grill flames up from the dripping fat, move the steaks to another spot. Turn

(Continued)

the steaks over and cook for an additional 8 minutes. After a total of 16 minutes, turn the steaks again and cook for 6 minutes on each side. At this point, continue to turn and cook each side for 6 minutes, or until the steaks reach an internal temperature of 120°F (medium-rare). Remove the steaks and allow them to rest for 10 minutes. Slice, top with the Herb Butter, sprinkle with sea salt and serve.

SUMMER GRILLING TIPS

Here are some of our tips and tricks for making your next grilling get-together an enjoyable and delicious experience.

- Select high quality meat with generous marbling (like USDA Prime) for maximum flavor.
- Have a high and low temperature area on your grill. Sometimes this is referred to as direct (high) and indirect (low) heating.
- Sear meats on the high heat, then finish on low.
- Keep a spray bottle filled with water handy to reduce flair ups. Charred meat does not taste very good.
- Leave the steak alone once they're on the grill. Allow the meat to caramelize on one side before turning.
- Never press down on your burgers. They're not going to cook any faster and all you're doing is squeezing out the juice and flavor.
- Don't cook sausage and franks over high heat. Their casings will burst, and the ground meat inside will lose its juiciness.
- When cooking an assortment of meat, begin with the thicker meats first like steaks, then add the burgers, then the sausage and franks so they all come off the grill at roughly the same time.
- Never put cooked meat back on the same platter the raw meat was on. Use a clean platter.
- Checking for doneness. This is not done by cutting or poking into the meat. Use a digital thermometer. To remind: Rare is when the internal temperature of the meat registers 120°F, Medium Rare: 130°F, Medium: 135°F, Medium Well: 145°F, and Well Done: 155°F. Keep in mind the internal temperature will continue to rise 5°F while the meat rests. Allowing the meat to rest before serving allows the juices to settle and reabsorb back into the meat (rather than spill out) resulting in a more flavorful bite.
- For maximum tenderness, always slice meat against the grain
- Brush the grill grates when you're finished cooking, and while the grill is still hot, for easier cleaning.

SIDES

SAUTÉED ZUCCHINI
WITH GARLIC CRUMBS

SERVES 4

GARLIC CRUMBS
MAKES 1½ CUPS

8 tablespoons unsalted butter
½ cup olive oil
1 cup panko breadcrumbs
8 cloves garlic, peeled and minced
1 shallot, peeled and minced
2 sprigs fresh thyme, chopped
1 sprig fresh rosemary, chopped
Kosher salt and fresh cracked black pepper, to taste

ZUCCHINI

3 green zucchinis, cut in fourths lengthwise
2 cloves garlic, peeled and finely chopped
2 sprigs finely chopped fresh thyme
Kosher salt and fresh cracked black pepper, to taste

Sautéed zucchini with garlic panko breadcrumbs is a simple yet flavorful dish. We slice fresh garden zucchini and top with a roasted garlic panko mixture, which adds a satisfying crunch with savory depth. We like this combination because it creates a balance between the tender zucchini and the crispy, garlicky breadcrumbs, making it a delicious side dish or a light main course that pairs well with many of our dishes in this chapter.

To make the Garlic Crumbs: Add the butter to a 2-quart saucepot over medium-high heat. Melt the butter until foaming. Add the olive oil followed by the panko, garlic, and shallot and stir in a figure 8 motion. The panko will soak up the fat and release it. Continue stirring with a wooden spoon, making sure to move the bottom and sides. Once the fat starts to release, you will begin to see foam again. Continue stirring for another 10 minutes, checking the color of the panko periodically by scooping some with the spoon. Once the panko reaches a golden brown, turn off the heat. Immediately toss in the chopped thyme and rosemary and continue stirring for 4 minutes. Strain, reserving the butter for later use. Once strained, place onto a baking sheet lined with a paper towel to catch any remaining fat. Serve immediately or store with a paper towel in the bottom of an airtight container.

To make the Zucchini: Preheat the oven to 350°F. Place the zucchini strips in a large bowl and add the Garlic Crumbs, garlic, thyme, reserved butter, salt and pepper. Toss well until the zucchini are well coated, then arrange them flat on a parchment lined baking sheet. Roast for 14 minutes and serve immediately.

ROASTED PEACHES
IN WHITE BORDEAUX

SERVES 4 TO 6

1 sprig fresh rosemary
2 Thai chilis, sliced in half
1 vanilla bean, split and
   scraped
4 ripe peaches, sliced in half
1½ cups sugar
6 tablespoons kosher salt
2 cups white Bordeaux wine
½ cup olive oil + more for
   drizzling the bread
4 slices sourdough bread
2 burrata cheese balls
¼ cup toasted almonds
2 tablespoons Saba vinegar
Pea shoots, as needed,
   optional

It always brings a smile to my face when I see Chef Brian returning from the Union Square Market with a bag full of ripe peaches. When we open the bag, we can smell the alluring fragrance of the fruit. We're like two children who just discovered a bag of treasured candy. We wait all year for times like this, and often we're disappointed with either mealy or bland peaches. Brian knows which farmers to get the best peaches and plums from, and they never disappoint. In this dish, the peaches are just magic. Even if the peaches you find aren't quite ready or sweet enough, roasting them will get them there rather quickly.

Preheat the oven to 350°F.

Add the rosemary, chilis, and vanilla to the bottom of a casserole dish followed by the peaches, flesh side up. Sprinkle the peaches with sugar and salt, making sure to cover each peach evenly. Gently pour the wine over each peach so the sugar and salt don't rinse off. Drizzle everything with olive oil and wrap the dish tightly with aluminum foil.

Bake for 30 minutes. Remove and carefully uncover. Allow to cool for 30 minutes. Note: To speed the cooling process, place in the refrigerator for 15 minutes.

To make the Grilled Sourdough: Drizzle olive oil on the slices. Grill over high heat until lightly charred. Turn, and grill until both sides are lightly charred. Remove and serve.

Once cooled, place the peaches and the juice into the desired serving dish. Arrange the burrata in the middle of the peaches. Sprinkle the toasted almonds and optional pea shoots on top, followed by a drizzle of Saba vinegar. Serve with a side of Grilled Sourdough.

DESSERT

PAVLOVA
WITH SUMMER FRUIT

MAKES 8 BAKED PAVLOVA

BAKED MERINGUE
1 cup egg whites
2 cups confectioners' sugar

SUMMER FRUIT
8 strawberries, hulled and
    quartered
1 cup blueberries
1 cup raspberries
1½ cups sugar
4 lemon thyme leaves
¼ cup champagne

CHANTILLY CREAM
1 cup heavy cream
¼ cup confectioners' sugar
½ teaspoon pure vanilla
    extract

LEMON CURD
¾ cup lemon juice
1½ tablespoon grated lemon
    zest
½ cup sugar
2 large eggs
4 large egg yolks
5 tablespoons unsalted butter

ZABAIONE
½ cup egg yolks
1 cup sugar
1 cup sweet wine (port,
    sherry, or marsala)

The famed pavlova, named after Russian ballerina, Anna Pavlova, in the early twentieth century, is a dessert is made from gently baked meringue and then filled with whipped cream and fresh fruit. Besides its pretty name, I like it for a couple of reasons: it's gluten free, which is important to many of our guests; it has fruit, which keeps the dish on the healthier side of our dessert offerings; it's very pretty; and it tastes great. You can customize your pavlova by using the seasonal fruit available to you. You can also fold a vanilla, chocolate, or mocha flavored pastry cream into the whipped cream. In this recipe, we fold in lemon curd for a bright touch of citrus.

To make the Baked Meringue: Preheat the oven to 225°F. Beat the egg whites until soft peaks begin to form. Gradually add half of the sugar. Once most of the sugar has folded into the egg whites, whip until stiff peaks form. Once stiff, fold in the remaining sugar. Remove the meringue from the bowl and transfer to a pastry or piping bag. On a lined baking sheet, pipe the meringue into 8 discs, measuring 4¼ inches in diameter, and keep 1 inch of space between each meringue. Bake for 2 to 3 hours, or until crisp but not browned. Remove and set aside to let cool.

To make the Summer Fruit: Add the strawberries, blueberries, raspberries, sugar, and thyme leaves to a medium mixing bowl. Gently mix to combine and set aside at room temperature for 20 minutes.

To make the Chantilly Cream: Add the cream to a mixing bowl and whip on medium speed until soft peaks form, 6 to 8 minutes. Add the sugar

(Continued)

and vanilla and continue whipping until stiff peaks form but still smooth. Be careful not to over-whip as this will cause the cream and milk solids to separate. Refrigerate until ready to use.

To make the Lemon Curd: Add the lemon juice, lemon zest, and sugar to a 2-quart saucepot. Stir to incorporate and place over medium heat. Bring to a simmer. Add the eggs and egg yolks to a mixing bowl and mix until combined. Gradually add the simmering lemon mixture to the egg mixture, while stirring constantly. Continuously mix to temper the eggs. Once the eggs have tempered, pour the mixture from the bowl back into the saucepot. Place over medium-low heat and cook, stirring continuously with a rubber spatula, until the mixture can coat the back of a spoon, about 6 to 8 minutes. Whisk in the butter until it has melted and incorporated evenly. Remove and allow to cool. Any extra can be stored in an airtight container in the refrigerator for up to 1 week.

To make the Zabaione: Add the egg yolks to a stainless-steel bowl. Using a whisk, beat the yolks until they start to foam. Add the sugar and wine and whisk until incorporated. Place the bowl over a double boiler and continue whisking until thick and silky, 3 to 4 minutes. Note: The mixture should look and feel a bit foamy.

Before serving, add the Chantilly Cream, Lemon Curd, and half of the Summer Fruit (add the champagne at this time) to a mixing bowl and mix to combine.

Arrange the Baked Meringues on the desired plates. Add the Chantilly Cream-Lemon Curd- Summer Fruit mixture to the top of the Meringues. Top with the Zabaione and the remaining Summer Fruit and serve.

SUMMER BERRY ZABAGLIONE

WITH LEMON LADY FINGERS

SERVES 4

LEMON LADY FINGERS
5 eggs, separated
1 cup sugar, divided
1 teaspoon lemon zest
1 cup sifted all-purpose flour
Powdered sugar, as needed

ZABAGLIONE
¾ cup prosecco or champagne
6 egg yolks
¼ cup sugar

ITALIAN MERINGUE
3 egg whites
1 cup sugar
2 tablespoons water

OTHER
Fresh blackberries,
   raspberries, blueberries, or
   strawberries, as desired

Pastry Chef Kerry's grandfather's side of the family is from Italy, so she wanted to add something to our menu that paid homage to her heritage. Summer is all about fresh and vibrant produce and this dessert showcases that. This is a simple dessert that packs a lot of refreshing flavors.

To make the Lemon Lady Fingers: Line a half sheet pan with parchment paper and set aside. Preheat the oven to 350°F. Add the egg yolks and ½ cup of sugar into a stand mixer with whisk attachment and whisk on medium speed until pale and thick. Set aside. Add the egg whites and the remaining ½ cup of sugar to a mixing bowl and whisk until soft peaks form. Gently fold in the egg white mixture and then fold in the lemon zest and sifted flour. Do not overmix. Place the mixture into a piping bag and pipe 3-inch lines. Dust them generously with powdered sugar. Bake for 10 minutes, or until lightly golden brown. Remove and set aside to cool.

To make the Zabaglione: Add the prosecco, egg yolks, and sugar to a mixing bowl. Place the bowl over a pot of simmering water (double boiler). Whisk constantly until the mixture reaches 200°F (use a candy or digital thermometer to check the temperature). Remove and place in the refrigerator to chill.

To make the Italian Meringue: Add the egg whites to a stand mixer with whisk attachment and whisk on high speed until the eggs are whipped. Next, add the sugar and water to a small pot over medium heat. Cook, stirring occasionally, until the sugar mixture reaches 240°F. Do not stir once the mixture comes to a boil or sugar crystals will develop. Once the sugar reaches temperature, turn the mixer on to medium speed and slowly stream in the hot sugar. Once all the sugar is in, turn the mixer back to high speed. Continue to mix until the egg whites are glossy. Remove the reserved Zabaglione from the refrigerator and fold into the Italian Meringue. Do not over mix or the mixture will deflate.

Transfer to individual dessert dishes and use a kitchen torch to lightly brown the Zabaglione. Alternatively, the same results can be achieved under a broiler. Serve chilled with fresh berries and the Lemon Lady Fingers.

AUTUMN

As a chef and native New Yorker, I find autumn the best time of year, beginning with the colorful grandeur of the fall foliage that paints the land in vibrant shades of yellow, orange, red, green, and brown. With that comes the cool dry air and the warm sun beaming from a bright blue sky. Everything is amazing on days like this. From a culinary standpoint, I look forward to apple and pumpkin picking and mushroom foraging. The markets, meanwhile, are filled with fruits, nuts, and plenty of fresh produce as well as wild game and an abundance of seafood, which come into season from the neighboring lakes, streams, and oceans. The cooler weather inspires heartier dishes through longer and slower cook times, bringing out the rich flavors of the season. In the kitchen, I enjoy adding fall ingredients like grapes, pears, pomegranate seeds, or a splash of cider vinegar to various meats, pastas, and vegetables to liven up the dish while balancing the richness of the heartier meal. Fall is also a time when I start using summer produce that I've preserved in the spring and summer. I'll pull out pickled ramps, stewed tomatoes, tomato water or corn for risotto, preserved kumquats, plum chutney, and much more. With so many wonderful flavors to play with, my team and I find it difficult to get them all on the menu.

GARDEN

BLACK MISSION FIG PIZZA

**SERVES 4 OR
4 (6 TO 8-INCH) PIZZAS**

**PIZZA DOUGH
MAKES 4 PERSONAL PIZZAS**

2 cups + 1½ tablespoons
    water
1½ tablespoons active dry
    yeast
1 tablespoon molasses
3¼ cups high-gluten flour
4 tablespoons olive oil
2 tablespoons kosher salt

**FIG JAM
MAKES 5 CUPS**

2 pounds Black Mission figs
1 cup sugar
¾ cup balsamic vinegar

TOPPINGS

2 cups Cheese Fondue
    (page 126)
1 cup Fig Jam
2 cups fresh mozzarella
    cheese, diced
8 to 10 fresh figs, quartered
4 ounces Spicy Coppa, thinly
    sliced
Arugula
Truffle oil
Freshly grated Parmesan
    cheese

As they say, a great pizza is all about the dough. At BLACKBARN, we've experimented with a number of different doughs, but we stand behind the one we've shared here. You really can't go wrong, especially when it serves as the base to this phenomenal pie made with Black Mission figs (see Ingredients and Pantry). The result is a pizza with a crunchy exterior dough that's soft on the inside and slathered with a bevy of cheese and seasonal toppings, offering a symphony of flavors and textures for any pizza lover.

To make the Pizza Dough: Add the water, yeast, and molasses to a standing mixer with the whisk attachment. Mix on medium speed until incorporated then allow the mixture to set for 10 minutes. Note: The mixture should foam, indicating the yeast has bloomed. Add the flour, oil, and salt. Replace the whisk attachment with the dough hook. Mix on low until a dough begins to form. Increase the speed to medium and continue kneading for 8 minutes. When finished, the elastic dough should be able to be stretched at least 2 inches without ripping or breaking. If breakage occurs, continue mixing in 2-minute intervals until the dough reaches the desired elasticity.

Transfer the dough to a medium bowl and cover with a damp kitchen towel. Place the dough in a warm area and allow to proof until it has doubled in size, 1 to 1½ hours. The time will vary depending on the room temperature.

Once proofed, divide the dough into 4 even balls. If a scale is handy, weigh the dough and divide by 4. Lightly flour the working surface and decide which side of the dough will be the top. Place the ball's top side down onto the working surface and begin pulling the outside up and to the center of each ball to smooth. Continue this step until the ball

(Continued)

that forms is completely smooth. When flipped over, it should have no cracks. Place the balls on a floured baking tray, cover them with a damp towel, and let them rest for 45 minutes.

To shape: Place a ball of dough on a floured surface. Starting from the middle and working towards the edge, press out the air, leaving about 1 inch of unpressed dough around the edges. You should only be using your fingertips for this step. Continue pressing out the air while rotating the dough clockwise and stretching simultaneously. An easy way to start is to use one hand to hold the dough in place and the other to stretch. Try drawing circles with your stretching hand. The dough should be stretched to 6 to 8 inches. Repeat the process with the remaining dough balls. They're now ready to top and bake in the oven.

To make the Fig Jam: Add the figs, sugar, and vinegar to a 2-quart saucepot over low heat. Gently mix to combine then cook for 1 hour and 10 minutes. Keep warm until ready to use. Refrigerate what is not used or preserve with a traditional canning method.

To make the Pizzas: Place a pizza stone in the oven and preheat it to 475°F. Cover each pizza with ¼ cup of Fig Jam and ½ cup of mozzarella. Spread ½ cup of Cheese Fondue over each pizza dough, leaving 1 inch of clean space around the edges. Place the pizza on the hot pizza stone in the middle of the oven. Bake for 12 minutes, then turn the pizza before baking for another 6 minutes, or until the crust is golden brown. Garnish with the fresh figs, spicy Coppa, arugula, a drizzle of truffle oil, and a sprinkle of Parmesan cheese. Cut into desired slices and serve.

HISTORY OF NEW YORK PIZZA

New York pizza, a culinary icon, has its roots in the late nineteenth and early twentieth centuries, brought to America by Italian immigrants. The first pizzeria in the United States, Lombardi's, opened in New York City in 1905, founded by Gennaro Lombardi, an immigrant from Naples. Lombardi's adapted the traditional Neapolitan pizza to suit American tastes and the availability of ingredients, using coal- or wood-fired ovens to create a crispier, smokier pizza that could be sold by the slice.

New York–style pizza is characterized by its large, thin, and foldable slices, with a slightly crispy crust and a simple topping of tomato sauce and mozzarella cheese. Over time, the style evolved, with pizzerias adding their own touches, such as a heavier hand with cheese and the introduction of various toppings. Here, at BLACKBARN, we specialize in seasonal toppings and our signature pizza dough.

In the post–World War II era, the popularity of pizza exploded across the United States, with New York pizza becoming a symbol of the city itself. It became a go-to food for busy New Yorkers, easy to eat on the go and relatively inexpensive. Today, New York–style pizza is celebrated worldwide, with countless pizzerias across the globe attempting to replicate its distinctive flavor and texture, maintaining its status as a beloved culinary tradition.

CUBAN-STYLE BLACK BEAN SOUP

SERVES 6 TO 8

BEANS
1 pound dried black beans

BOUQUET GARNI
2 to 3 sprigs fresh thyme
2 to 3 sprigs fresh rosemary
2 to 3 sprigs fresh Italian flatleaf parsley
2 bay leaves

SOUP
2 tablespoons olive oil
1 cup diced Spanish onion
⅔ cup diced celery
⅔ cup diced red pepper
⅔ cup diced carrot
3 cloves garlic, minced
4 teaspoons ground cumin
1 tablespoon ground
coriander
cayenne to taste
8 cups vegetable stock
1 teaspoon salt
2 tablespoons lime juice
2 tablespoons minced fresh
cilantro

GARNISH
6 to 8 tablespoons of Pico de
Gallo (see page 220)

FRIED TORTILLA STRIPS
3 cups coconut or avocado oil
for frying
2 corn tortillas, cut in ¼- x
2-inch strips

Here is the meatless version of the most popular soup from my years at the Waldorf Astoria. So hearty and delicious, it's practically a meal in and of itself, but I usually enjoy it at lunch with a Turkey Club sandwich.

To make the Beans: Place the beans in a large bowl, add 4 cups cold water or enough to cover the beans by at least 1 inch, and let soak overnight. The next day, drain the beans and rinse under cold running water. Set aside.

To make the Bouquet Garni: Tie a small bundle of thyme, rosemary, parsley, and two bay leaves with twine.

To make the Soup: Heat olive oil in a large saucepan over medium-low heat and sauté the onions and celery for 3 to 4 minutes until tender, stirring often. Add the red pepper, carrot, and garlic and cook for about 3 more minutes. Add the cumin, coriander, and cayenne, and stir well. Add the bouquet garni, drained black beans, vegetable stock, salt, and bring to a boil. Turn the heat to low and simmer until the beans are tender, about $1\frac{1}{2}$ hours. Add a little more stock or water if the soup gets too thick.

To make the Fried Tortilla Strips: Heat the frying oil in a saucepan to 350°F. Test the heat by placing a tortilla strip in the pan. If the strip immediately bubbles and fries, the oil is hot enough. Add the tortilla strips and deep-fry for 15 to 20 seconds, until golden brown. Remove them with a slotted spoon, drain on paper towels, and season with a pinch of salt.

Remove the bouquet garni from the soup and stir in the lime juice and minced cilantro. Pour the soup into warm serving bowls and garnish each serving with 1 tablespoon of Pico de Gallo. Sprinkle the fried tortilla strips on top and serve.

CURRIED CAULIFLOWER STEAKS

WITH LEMON DRESSING AND PICKLED RAISINS

SERVES 6

RAITA SAUCE
MAKES 2 CUPS

1 cup plain Greek full-fat
   yogurt
¼ cup peeled and chopped red
   onion
2 tablespoons chopped
   cilantro
1 tablespoon lime juice
2 tablespoons lemon juice
¼ teaspoon ground coriander
¼ teaspoon ground cumin
½ teaspoon fresh cracked
   black pepper
$1/8$ teaspoon ground nutmeg
$1/8$ teaspoon ground cinnamon
$1/8$ teaspoon ground
   cardamom
Sea salt, to taste

PICKLED RAISINS
MAKES 2½ CUPS

3 cups white wine vinegar
1 cup sugar
3 tablespoons kosher salt
1 cup golden raisins

CAULIFLOWER STEAKS

3 medium cauliflower heads
4 tablespoons curry powder
Sea salt and fresh cracked
   black pepper, to taste
6 tablespoons olive oil, divided
3 tablespoons unsalted butter,
   divided
3 cloves garlic, peeled, divided
6 sprigs fresh thyme, divided

Before developing the opening menu for BLACKBARN, I knew it would lean heavy on meat so having great vegetarian dishes was a must. This dish was created to meet that need, but it has exceeded all expectations. The rich and cooling Raita Sauce, made from full-fat Greek yogurt, complements the warm spices of the cauliflower steaks, which are enhanced by a crisp sear and infused with the subtle earthiness of thyme and garlic. It was an immediate hit and remains on the menu to this day.

To make the Raita Sauce: Add the yogurt, onion, cilantro, lime and lemon juice, coriander, cumin, pepper, nutmeg, cinnamon, and cardamom to a medium-sized bowl. Mix well to combine and season with salt. Let sit at room temperature for at least 40 minutes before use. If not using immediately, cover and store in the refrigerator for up to 1 week. Let the sauce reach room temperature before using.

To make the Pickled Raisins: Add the vinegar, sugar, and salt to a 1-quart saucepot over high heat and bring to a boil. Remove from the heat and immediately add the raisins. Cover the pot with a lid and allow to cool at room temperature for at least 2 hours before serving.

To make the Cauliflower: Preheat the oven to 350°F. Using a cutting board, clean the cauliflowers and slice 2 (2-inch thick) center-cut "steaks" from each cauliflower head, and season with curry powder, salt, and pepper. Place a sauté pan on the stove over medium heat and add 2 tablespoons of olive oil, 1 tablespoon of butter, 1 clove of garlic, 1 sprig of thyme, and 2 cauliflower steaks. Reduce the heat to low and cook the cauliflower until golden brown on each side, about 2 minutes. Transfer the steaks to a sheet pan. Repeat the process with the remaining steaks. Once all steaks have been prepared, roast them in the oven for 25 minutes or until a knife can be inserted without resistance.

GARDEN GREEN SALAD
1 head romaine lettuce, chopped
½ head radicchio
1 cup cucumber, sliced into 1/3-inch strips
2 cups grape tomatoes, cut in half
20 cilantro leaves, chopped
4 tablespoons toasted pine nuts
7 tablespoons Lemon Dressing (page 108)
Sea salt, to taste

In the meantime, prepare the Lemon Dressing (page 108).

Prepare the Garden Green Salad by adding the lettuce, radicchio, cucumber, tomatoes, cilantro, and pine nuts to a large bowl. Lightly toss with the Lemon Dressing and season with salt.

Pour a spoonful of Raita Sauce on each plate (plates should be large, about 11 inches). Place 1 piece of warm cauliflower steak on top of the sauce. Garnish with the salad, top with the Pickled Raisins, and serve.

🍷 Wine Suggestion
Sauvignon Blanc, Pouilly Fumé, France

BUTTERNUT SQUASH RAVIOLI

WITH SAGE BEURRE MONTÉ

SERVES 6

PASTA DOUGH
2 cups "00" flour
2 tablespoons semolina flour
2 whole eggs
3 egg yolks

PUMPKIN SEEDS
1 cup pumpkin seeds
½ teaspoon paprika
3 tablespoons maple syrup
2 tablespoons olive oil
Kosher salt and fresh cracked
  black pepper, to taste

FILLING
1 large butternut squash
2 tablespoons olive oil
Kosher salt and white pepper,
  to taste
4 tablespoons crumbled
  amaretto cookies
8 tablespoons freshly grated
  Parmesan cheese
2 teaspoons ground nutmeg
4 tablespoons small diced fruit
  mostarda (candied spicy fruit)
Egg Wash (page 98)

SAGE BEURRE MONTÉ
1 cup heavy cream
1 stick (8 tablespoons)
  unsalted butter, cubed
6 sage leaves
Kosher salt to taste

SWISS CHARD AND BACON
2 bunches Swiss chard
1 shallot, peeled and chopped
3 thick slices bacon
2 tablespoons olive oil

When we first opened BLACKBARN, Chef Matteo Bergamini was the chef, and Chef Brian Fowler was the Sous Chef. Matteo is a fantastic chef and an Italian native who brought several outstanding dishes to life to the restaurant. One such standout is our Butternut Squash Ravioli which has salty-sweet notes, and a chewy texture with crunchy spiced pepitas. Our pastas are always a hit with our guests, and the Butternut Squash Ravioli is one of the most requested—guests will come in for that dish alone. We like to serve this dish with bacon lardons, but it's equally wonderful without the bacon. The dish is also perfect for entertaining because you can make the ravioli ahead of time and freeze them until you are ready to eat.

To make the Pasta Dough: Add the flours, eggs, and yolks to a stand mixer with the dough hook attachment. Mix until a homogenous dough has formed. Pull the dough from the bowl and place on a floured surface. Cover with a damp towel and allow to rest for 30 minutes. Note: You can prepare the pasta dough the day before and store in the refrigerator, covered with plastic wrap until ready to use.

To make the Pumpkin Seeds: Preheat the oven to 385°F. Add the pumpkin seeds to a medium-sized mixing bowl along with the paprika, syrup, and olive oil. Mix well and season with salt and pepper. Spread the mixture evenly on a lined baking sheet and place in the oven for 8 minutes. Remove and use a rubber spatula or wooden spoon to gently move the pumpkin seeds around. Return to the oven another 6 minutes, or until the seeds puff just a bit. Remove and set aside.

To make the Filling: Preheat the oven to 350°F. Peel the squash, cut in half lengthwise, and remove the seeds. Cut the squash into 2-inch cubes, place them on a baking sheet, and season with olive oil, salt, and pepper. Bake for 40 minutes, or until fork tender. Remove, let cool

(Continued)

for 20 minutes, and then pass through a food mill. Place the squash purée in a bowl and add the amaretto cookies, Parmesan, nutmeg, and diced fruit mostarda. Mix well, check and adjust the taste if needed, and refrigerate until ready to use.

To make the Ravioli: Roll out the pasta dough very thin and cut out 30, 3-inch square pieces. Place 1½ tablespoons of the filling in the middle of each square and brush with the Egg Wash. Fold it, bringing each corner to the center like a pyramid. Press the borders firmly together. Arrange the ravioli on a tray with parchment paper dusted with flour until you are ready to cook them.

To make the Sage Beurre Monté: Add the cream to a 2-quart saucepan over medium heat and simmer. Whisk in the butter one piece at a time. Add the sage and let the sauce reduce for several minutes at a simmer. Season to taste with salt, remove from the heat, and set aside.

To make the Swiss Chard and Bacon: Rinse the chard and remove the stems. Dry the leaves and cut into 1-inch-wide strips. Add the oil to a sauté pan over medium heat. When the oil is shimmering, add the shallots. Cook the shallots until translucent then add the chard. When the leaves have wilted, remove and set aside. Next, slice the bacon into small (⅓-inch) pieces and caramelize the bacon in the sauté pan over medium heat for 10 minutes, or until golden brown and crispy. Remove and set aside.

To cook the Ravioli: Bring 4 quarts of salted water to a boil over high heat. Gently remove the reserved ravioli from the tray and place them in the boiling water. Cook for 4 minutes or until they float. Remove and drain the ravioli with a skimmer and arrange them on a serving platter or dishes. Spoon the Sage Beurre Monté over the ravioli and sprinkle with Parmesan cheese.

Divide the Swiss Chard on individual serving plates and place the ravioli on top. Garnish with more Parmesan cheese, a few pieces of the crispy bacon and toasted pumpkin seeds, and serve.

🍷 Wine Suggestion
Chardonnay, Russian River Valley, USA

OCEAN

LIVE DAY BOAT SCALLOP CRUDO
WITH CAVIAR CHIVE VINAIGRETTE

SERVES 4 TO 6

1½ pounds fresh U10 dry
   scallops (see sizing,
   page 191)
Sea salt, to taste

CAVIAR CHIVE VINAIGRETTE
MAKES ½ CUP

1 tablespoon Moscatel vinegar
1 tablespoon white wine
   vinegar
⅛ teaspoon Dijon mustard
1 teaspoon sea salt
¼ teaspoon white pepper
6 tablespoons olive oil
1 tablespoon paddlefish caviar
1 tablespoon trout roe
2 tablespoons minced chives

Fresh scallops and caviar are a fabulous combination that brings back fond memories. I remember preparing a State Dinner at the Waldorf Hotel hosted by President Clinton. I seared the scallops in olive oil, butter, and thyme and served them with a caviar chive vinaigrette. Today, when we can get the sweetest day boat scallops, I can't resist serving the succulent treats raw with salty caviar and a slightly acidic vinaigrette. Try it and you'll experience the true essence of the sea on your palate.

With a sharp knife, slice each scallop into 3 even medallions. Arrange 5 to 6 slices on each plate.

To make the Caviar Chive Vinaigrette: Add the vinegars and mustard to a small mixing bowl. Whisk together to combine. Add the salt and pepper. Drizzle in the olive oil while whisking vigorously until all ingredients have emulsified. Add the caviar, roe, and chives.

Spoon it over the scallops and sprinkle with sea salt to serve.

CRISP-SKINNED STRIPED BASS

WITH CORN RISOTTO AND CHANTERELLE MUSHROOMS

SERVES 8

CORN PURÉE
MAKES 1¼ CUPS

3 tablespoons olive oil
1 large shallot, peeled and minced
1 clove garlic, peeled and smashed
3 fresh thyme sprigs
1 cup summer corn kernels
¼ cup whole milk
¼ cup heavy cream

CHANTERELLE MUSHROOMS

2 tablespoons olive oil
½ pound chanterelle mushrooms, cleaned
1 shallot, minced
3 fresh thyme sprigs
2 tablespoons sherry vinegar
Kosher salt and fresh cracked black pepper

CORN RISOTTO

1½ quarts Homemade Vegetable Stock (page 172)
6 tablespoons olive oil
12 tablespoons cold butter, divided
½ cup peeled and small-diced Spanish onion
2 bay leaves
1 cup carnaroli or arborio rice
1 cup white wine (Chardonnay or Sauvignon Blanc)
½ cup grated fresh Parmesan cheese

In part due to our Long Island roots, both Chef Brian and I enjoy heading out to sea to bring back some beautiful striped bass. No matter their size—and we've landed some whoppers—the battle on rod and reel is always worth the trip. Best of all, those gorgeous stripers end up at the dinner table. For this recipe, we like to get the skin very crispy while the flesh remains tender and juicy with a subtle hint of the sea. Our favorite preparation at BLACKBARN is with our sweet Corn Risotto and Chanterelle Mushrooms. Striped bass, like chicken, is quite versatile and can lend itself to many different flavors, including red wine sauces, but be careful not to use ingredients that will overpower or conflict with its delicate flavor. As a chef once told me, "Simplicity is the mother of beauty!"

To make the Corn Purée: Add the olive oil to a 1-quart saucepot over medium-high heat. When heated, add the shallots, garlic, and thyme. Cook until fragrant, about 4 to 6 minutes. Add the corn, milk, and cream. Bring to a boil then reduce the heat to low and let simmer for 3 to 5 minutes. Using an immersion or standing blender, blend until smooth. Transfer to an airtight container and set aside until ready to use or store in the refrigerator for up to 1 week.

To make the Chanterelle Mushrooms: Add the olive oil to a 10-inch skillet over high heat. When the oil is heated, add the mushrooms and cook until the mushrooms release water, about 6 minutes. Continue cooking until 80% of the water has evaporated. Add the shallots and thyme and sauté for an additional 2 minutes. Season with sherry vinegar and salt and pepper to taste. Set aside until ready to use or store in an airtight container in the refrigerator for up to 1 week.

(Continued)

1 cup Corn Purée
Sea salt and fresh cracked
  black pepper, to taste

STRIPED BASS
2 tablespoons olive oil
8 (6-ounce) ocean striped
  bass filets
Kosher salt and white pepper,
  to taste
2 tablespoons unsalted butter
2 cloves garlic, peeled and
  quartered
8 sprigs fresh thyme
2 strips lemon peel

To make the Corn Risotto: Add the vegetable stock to a 2-quart saucepot over medium heat. Bring it to a light simmer, but not a boil. Keep on medium heat for a later step.

Add the olive oil and 4 tablespoons of cold butter to a 12-inch sauté pan over medium-high heat. When the butter is foaming, add the onions and bay leaves. Cook until the onions are translucent, about 4 minutes. Add the rice and lightly toast in the pan for 6 minutes, stirring occasionally with a wooden spoon. After 6 minutes, add the white wine and continue to cook until the alcohol aroma has dissipated, about 8 minutes.

Lower the heat to medium and ladle enough hot vegetable stock to just cover the rice. Continue cooking and stirring the rice with a wooden spoon until the stock evaporates. Add more hot stock to just cover the rice again and stir. Continue this process until the rice is "al dente" and most of the stock is absorbed, about 20 minutes to cook rice fully.

Once the rice has cooked, reduce the heat to low and add the remaining cold butter, Parmesan, and Corn Purée. With a wooden spoon, continue stirring the rice until the butter is no longer visible. Remove bay leaves. Season with salt and pepper.

To make the Striped Bass: Preheat the oven to 325°F. Add 1 tablespoon olive oil to a 10- to 12-inch skillet over medium-high heat. When heated, add 4 of the fish filets, skin side down, and season with salt and pepper. Sear for 3 minutes then add 1 tablespoon of butter. Add 4 quarters of garlic, 4 sprigs of thyme, and 1 piece of lemon peel. Cook the fish for several minutes, basting it with the butter and oil from the pan until the skin is browned and crisp. Transfer the fish to a baking sheet with the skin side up and repeat the cooking process with the remaining filets. When all the filet skins are browned, place them on a baking sheet and bake until the fish is cooked through, about 3 to 4 minutes, depending on the thickness of the fish.

Evenly distribute the Corn Risotto across individual serving plates. Top with one fish filet. Garnish with Chantarelle Mushrooms and serve.

🍷 Wine Suggestion
Sangiovese, Rosso di Montalcino, Tuscany, Italy

PAUPIETTES OF DOVER SOLE
WITH SHRIMP MOUSSELINE, SEA BEANS, AND CAVIAR-CHIVE SAUCE

SERVES 4

SHRIMP MOUSSELINE
1 pound raw shrimp, peeled and deveined
Kosher salt and white pepper, to taste
½ cup heavy cream
1 large egg
6 sprigs fresh Italian flat leaf parsley, chopped
8 chives, chopped
2 sprigs fresh mint, chopped
2 whole (18- to 22-ounce) Dover Sole fish, fileted
Unsalted butter, for coating
2 shallots, minced
¼ cup white wine

BLONDE ROUX
½ tablespoon unsalted butter
½ tablespoon all-purpose flour

SEA BEANS
2 cups sea beans (or haricot verts)

HOMEMADE FISH STOCK
MAKES 2½ CUPS
1 pound fish bones and/or heads, rinsed clean
2 to 3 Spanish onions, peeled and thinly sliced
¼ fennel bulb, thinly sliced
½ stalk celery
1 clove garlic, peeled and crushed
½ teaspoon whole black peppercorns

Regardless of how it's prepared, I love dover sole. With its firm texture and delicate flavor, this fish is a slice of seafood heaven. I particularly enjoy this preparation because we use the bones to make a delicious stock and sauce in which we mix some caviar and chives. We then add a layer of fish mousse with shrimp and herbs in between, delivering yet another sliver of flavor and texture. The caviar, of course, offers little pops of saltiness when you press them against the roof of your mouth, making this a truly divine dish.

To make the Shrimp Mousseline: Add the shrimp, salt, and pepper to a food processor. Blend until a rough chop forms. With the machine still on, add the heavy cream and fully incorporate. Add the egg and mix until smooth. Transfer the mixture to a medium bowl and, using a rubber spatula, fold in the parsley, chives, and mint. Scrape the sides of the bowl and transfer the mixture into a piping bag.

Preheat the oven to 325°F.

Pipe an even ½-inch thick layer of Mousseline onto 4 dover sole filets. Stack the remaining 4 filets on top of the Mousseline.

Coat the bottom of a deep-dish casserole with unsalted butter and minced shallots. Carefully place the stuffed filets in the casserole, leaving as much space as possible between them. Pour the white wine into the dish and cover tightly with aluminum foil. Bake for 24 minutes.

While the fish is cooking, make the Blonde Roux. Add the butter to a sauté pan and melt over medium heat. Use a wooden spoon to fold the flour into the butter. Cook for 2 to 3 minutes. Once the butter and flour are combined, the mixture should resemble wet sand. Remove from the heat and set aside.

(Continued)

2 bay leaves
5 sprigs fresh thyme
1 bottle (750 ml) dry
    white wine

CAVIAR-CHIVE SAUCE
MAKES ¾ CUP
2½ cups Homemade Fish Stock
1 cup heavy cream
1 tablespoon Blonde Roux
Kosher salt and white pepper,
    to taste
1½ tablespoons paddlefish
    caviar
1½ tablespoons salmon roe
1 tablespoon chopped fresh
    chives

To make the Sea Beans: Place the beans in a pot of boiling, salted water for 15 seconds. Strain and immediately submerge in an ice water bath for 30 seconds. Remove from the ice water and set aside.

To make the Homemade Fish Stock: Add the bones and heads to an 8-quart pot over high heat. Add the onions, fennel, celery, garlic, peppercorns, bay leaves, and thyme. Add enough wine to just cover the contents. Bring to a boil, then reduce heat to medium-low to maintain an even, gentle simmer. Let simmer for 40 minutes, strain through a chinois, and set aside.

To make the Caviar-Chive Sauce: Add the Homemade Fish Stock and cream to a 1-quart saucepot over medium heat. Bring to a low simmer and reduce to about 1 cup. Whisk in the Blonde Roux until all the lumps have dissolved. Simmer for an additional 10 minutes. Once the fish has finished cooking, add the strained juice from the cooked dover sole to the sauce and simmer until it is thick enough to coat the back of a spoon. Mix in the caviar, trout roe, and chives.

Arrange the Sea Beans on serving plates. Transfer the dover sole from the casserole dish onto a cutting board. Using a kitchen knife, cut the sole in half lengthwise, exposing the Mousseline. Pour the Caviar Chive Sauce around the fish filets and serve.

🍷 Wine Suggestion
Crisp Viognier, Washington State, USA

PASTURE

EIGHT-HOUR BARBECUE BEEF RIBS

WITH CHIPOTLE-ORANGE SPICE RUB

SERVES 4 TO 6

3 (7-rib) Back Rib Racks
Chipotle-Orange Spice Rub
(page 134), as needed
Kosher salt, to taste
Barbecue Sauce (page 138)

In the 1980s, most of the guests attending the Waldorf Astoria's Grand Ballroom events would request prime rib. And every evening, when those massive seven-rib roasts were pulled from the oven, we'd remove the rack of bones before slicing and set the ribs aside for staff meals the following day. Personally, I've never cared much for prime rib, as I find the cut lacks the rich flavor of the caramelized char that comes from grilling. However, what I do love is the tender succulent meat between those rib bones. I remember telling myself when I was carving those roasts at the Waldorf, that when I open a restaurant one day, I'll buy just the rib bones and cook them until they fall off the bone for my guests to enjoy. Today, that's exactly what we've done. These eight-hour beef ribs are one of the most popular items on the BLACKBARN menu. Nothing makes me happier then when someone from Texas (who is very proud of their ribs) dines with us and claims, "These are the best I've ever had!"

Preheat the oven to 250°F.

Divide the racks so that a set of 3 bones have meat attached at either end, discarding the single bones from the middle that now have no meat. Generously season the meat on all sides with the Chipotle-Orange Spice Rub and salt. Place the seasoned ribs (meat side up) in a roasting pan. Pour 1-inch of water into the pan, just touching the bottom of the ribs, and cover tightly with aluminum foil. Place in the oven and cook for 8 hours, or until the ribs are fork tender. Note: A knife should be able to pass through the meat easily when finished. Remove the aluminum foil, brush the ribs with Barbecue Sauce, and serve.

🍷 Wine Suggestion
Carmenere, Colchagua Valley, Chile

DUCK BREAST PASTRAMI
WITH ROASTED PARSNIPS AND SWEET AND SOUR SHALLOTS

SERVES 4

DUCK
2 (11-ounce) premium
   boneless duck breasts
   with skin-on

PASTRAMI SPICE CURE
MAKES ½ CUP
5 tablespoons kosher salt
1½ tablespoons fresh cracked
   black pepper
2 tablespoons ground
   coriander
1½ teaspoons ground nutmeg
2 teaspoons ground cloves

PASTRAMI BRINE
MAKES 4 CUPS
4 cups water
1½ tablespoons kosher salt
4 bay leaves
1 teaspoon white wine

ROASTED PARSNIPS
3 parsnips, cleaned and
   quartered
1 tablespoon olive oil
3 sprigs fresh thyme
Sea salt and fresh cracked
   black pepper, to taste

SWEET AND SOUR SHALLOTS
1 cup sugar
1 cup Moscatel vinegar (see
   Ingredients and Pantry)
3 tablespoons water
4 bay leaves
6 medium shallots, peeled and
   cut in half
2 tablespoons sea salt

Duck pastrami is an idea that Chef Brian Fowler had talked about creating for some time. When our seasonal menu needed to be changed, he seized the moment. We hear from our guests all the time that the dish is the best duck they've ever had. The smoke and spices pair so well with the sweet tender duck breast. Although this recipe may look complicated because of the extra steps involved, it's quite easy and the curing and brining can be done days prior to cooking and serving. This dish is also excellent to serve year-round. One word of caution: don't overcook the duck. Once the breast goes past medium, it tends to dry out.

To make the Pastrami Spice Cure: Add the salt, pepper, coriander, nutmeg, and cloves to a medium-sized bowl. Mix well then season the flesh side of the duck breasts with the mixture. Transfer the duck breasts, fat-side up, to a 6 × 9 baking dish with at least a 1-inch depth. Refrigerate for 4 hours, up to 24 hours.

To make the Pastrami Brine: Add the water, salt, bay leaves, and wine to a 1-quart pot over high heat and bring to a boil. Remove and let cool. Pour the brine into the dish with the duck breasts, stopping where the fat begins. Cover and refrigerate again for 4 hours, up to 24 hours. Remove the duck breasts from the brine and blot dry with paper towels.

To make the Roasted Parsnips: Preheat the oven to 350°F. On a half-sheet pan, coat the quartered parsnips with olive oil, thyme, salt, and pepper. Roast until tender and lightly browned on the edges, 14 to 16 minutes. Remove and let cool slightly before serving.

To make the Sweet and Sour Shallots: Add the sugar, vinegar, and water to a 1-quart pot over high heat. Bring to a boil and then reduce to a simmer. Add the bay leaves, shallots, and salt. Cook until the shallots are fork tender, about 15 minutes. Keep warm until ready to use. Remove bay leaves.

(Continued)

BLACKBARN

FINISHING SPICE
MAKES ¼ CUP

3 tablespoons coarse ground
black pepper
1½ tablespoons coriander
seed
1½ tablespoons mustard seed

To make the Finishing Spice: Use a mortar and pestle to crush the pepper and seeds until coarsely ground. Distribute the finishing spice evenly over the fat side of the duck breasts.

To make the Duck: Add the duck breasts, fat side down, to a 9- to 12-inch skillet. Over medium-low heat, render the fat without burning until the duck is golden brown, about 15 minutes. With a spoon, remove any excess fat throughout the rendering process until all the fat has been discarded (you'll do this about 3 times). Turn the duck breasts to flesh-side-down. Continue cooking until the duck is medium rare or the internal temperature registers 125° to 130°F. Divide each breast into 2 portions. Serve with the Roasted Parsnips and Sweet and Sour Shallots.

🍷 Wine Suggestion
Tempranillo, Rioja, Spain

FARMED VS WILD DUCK

Farmed and wild ducks differ significantly in their lifestyle, diet, and flavor. Farmed ducks are raised in controlled environments where their diet and living conditions are managed to optimize growth and production. They are typically fed a consistent diet of grains and protein supplements, leading to a more predictable flavor and texture. Farmed ducks are often kept in confined spaces, which can affect their overall health and quality of meat.

In contrast, wild ducks roam freely in natural habitats like wetlands, rivers, and lakes. Their diet varies based on the available natural resources, including aquatic plants, insects, and small fish. This diverse diet contributes to a more complex, gamey flavor and firmer texture in wild duck meat. Wild ducks also experience a more active lifestyle, which can affect the meat's tenderness and fat distribution.

While farmed duck offers consistency and easier availability, wild duck is prized for its unique taste and natural, varied diet. The choice between them often depends on personal preference and desired flavor profile.

SIDES

ROASTED ACORN SQUASH
WITH APPLE-GINGER BUTTER

SERVES 4

APPLE GINGER BUTTER
MAKES 2 CUPS

1 Gala apple, peeled, quartered and seeded
1¼ cups apple cider
1½ teaspoons ground cinnamon
1 star anise
⅛ teaspoon ground nutmeg
4 tablespoons dark brown sugar
1-inch piece ginger, peeled
1 cup unsalted butter, softened
Kosher salt, to taste

ROASTED ACORN SQUASH

2 acorn squash, cut in eighths
2 sprigs fresh sage
1 sprig fresh rosemary
3 cloves garlic, peeled and smashed
5 tablespoons olive oil
Kosher salt and fresh cracked black pepper, to taste
1½ cups pomegranate seeds

Roasted acorn squash with apple ginger butter is a cozy, flavorful autumn dish. The sweet, nutty flavor of the roasted squash pairs beautifully with the tangy, spiced apple ginger butter. Simply spoon the butter over the warm squash for a sweet-savory combination that's perfect as a light, comforting meal or as a side dish for poultry or wild game.

To make the Apple Ginger Butter: Add the apple, cider, cinnamon, star anise, nutmeg, brown sugar, and ginger to a 1-quart saucepot over medium-high heat. Bring to a boil then reduce the heat to medium-low and allow to simmer until the Gala apple has softened just enough to almost break apart, about 8 minutes. Remove from the heat and allow to cool.

Mix the apple mixture and softened butter in a food processor until blended. Reserve until needed.

Preheat the oven to 365°F.

Add the acorn squash, sage, rosemary, garlic, olive oil, salt, and pepper to a medium-sized mixing bowl. Coat and season each piece of squash evenly. Place on a lined baking sheet. Roast uncovered on the middle rack for 26 minutes. Remove and set aside.

Add ½ cup of Apple Ginger Butter to a 10-inch sauté pan over medium heat. Once melted, remove and spoon over the reserved acorn squash. Garnish with pomegranate seeds and serve.

DESSERT

APPLE CIDER DOUGHNUTS
WITH CARAMEL SAUCE

SERVES 4 TO 6

APPLE CIDER DOUGHNUTS
MAKES ABOUT 20 MINI
 DOUGHNUTS
1 cup softened unsalted
 butter
3½ cups sugar
6 eggs
¾ cup buttermilk
1¼ cups apple cider
8½ cups all-purpose flour
3 teaspoons kosher salt
5 teaspoons baking powder
4 teaspoons baking soda
2½ teaspoons ground
 cinnamon
⅛ teaspoon ground nutmeg
5 Granny Smith apples, peeled
 and shredded
6 cups coconut oil for deep
 frying

CINNAMON SUGAR
MAKES ABOUT ¾ CUP
1 tablespoon ground
 cinnamon
¾ cup sugar

CARAMEL SAUCE
MAKES 1 CUP
⅓ cup sugar
1 teaspoon water
¼ cup unsalted butter
⅓ cup heavy cream
1 teaspoon kosher salt

Does anyone not love warm doughnuts? Growing up, I craved the warm, out-of-the-fryer doughnuts that were available at the local farm stands near my home. Today, in New York, I can find some creative and delicious doughnuts, but none of them are ever warm. Serving warm doughnuts was a must for me when I opened BLACKBARN, and I'm glad I do it. When you order these little bites of heaven, we make them to order and they arrive tableside still warm with a gooey caramel sauce that's absolutely addictive.

To make the Doughnuts: Add the softened butter and sugar to a stand mixer with paddle attachment. Mix on medium speed until a cream forms, about 4 minutes. Add the eggs, one at a time, waiting until each egg is completely incorporated before adding the next egg. Add the buttermilk and the apple cider and continue to mix. Add the flour, salt, baking powder, baking soda, cinnamon, and nutmeg, and continue to mix until well combined. Once a homogenous dough has formed, add the shredded apples and mix until evenly distributed.

Transfer the dough to a lightly floured work surface. Using a rolling pin, roll the dough to a ¼-inch thickness. Transfer to a parchment lined baking sheet and refrigerate for 4 hours. Note: If the dough does not fit on your sheet, trim the dough or separate onto 2 sheets.

While the dough is refrigerated, make the Cinnamon Sugar mixture and Caramel Sauce.

To make the Cinnamon Sugar: Add the cinnamon and sugar to a bowl and mix until combined. Set aside until ready to use.

(Continued)

To make the Caramel Sauce: Add the sugar and water to a 1-quart saucepot. Mix with a wooden spoon until the mixture resembles wet sand and forms a flat, even layer in the bottom of the pot. Note: Don't stir too much. Now turn on the heat to medium-high. Allow the mixture to warm until the sugar dissolves, turns clear, and starts to bubble, 3 to 4 minutes. Do not stir at this stage as this will cause the sugar to crystallize. Swirl the pan, brushing down the sides with a pastry brush dipped in water as needed until the mixture thickens and turns a deep amber color, 8 to 12 minutes. Be careful not to let the sugar burn during this step. Add the butter and whisk until the butter has completely melted. Remove the pot from the heat and gradually pour in the heavy cream and salt while continuing to whisk. Let cool for 10 minutes before serving. If not using right away, store in an airtight container in the refrigerator for up to 2 weeks.

In a 3-quart saucepot over medium-high heat, bring the coconut oil up to 375°F. Use a candy or digital thermometer to check the temperature.

Remove the dough from the refrigerator. Use a 2-inch diameter cookie cutter, press circles into the flat dough, leaving them in place. Using a 1-inch diameter cookie cutter, cut out the center of each previously formed circle, creating the doughnut shape. Note: The small 1-inch circles removed from the center can be used for doughnut holes or combined with the excess clippings to be rolled out again. Repeat the process until all dough has been used. Deep fry immediately or freeze the dough in an airtight container for up to 2 months.

To fry the doughnuts: Gently place the doughnuts into the hot oil. The doughnuts will sink to the bottom at first, but after about 15 seconds they will float to the top. Once floating, allow them to cook for 1 minute 30 seconds. Use a fork to gently flip them over and cook the other side for another 1 minute 30 seconds.

Remove the doughnuts and drain on a paper towel-lined tray. Gently toss the doughnuts into the Cinnamon Sugar mixture until well coated and serve immediately with the Caramel Sauce either drizzled on top or on the side.

PUMPKIN CHEESECAKE
WITH GINGERSNAP COOKIE CRUST

SERVES 6 TO 8

PUMPKIN CHEESECAKE

4½ cups softened cream cheese

¾ cup sugar

¼ cup dark brown sugar

1 vanilla bean, split and scraped

3 large eggs

2¼ cups canned pumpkin purée

1 tablespoon ground cinnamon

⅛ teaspoon ground nutmeg

¼ teaspoon ground cloves

⅛ teaspoon ground ginger

GINGERSNAP COOKIES

¾ cup unsalted butter

½ cup dark brown sugar

6 tablespoons sugar

1 tablespoon grated fresh ginger

5 tablespoons molasses

½ teaspoon pure vanilla extract

1 large egg

½ teaspoon baking soda

¼ teaspoon kosher salt

2 teaspoons ground ginger

1½ teaspoons ground cinnamon

¼ teaspoon ground cloves

1 ½ cups all-purpose flour

GINGER SNAP CRUST

Gingersnap Cookies (recipe above)

1½ cups unsalted butter, melted

1 cup dark brown sugar

3 tablespoons kosher salt

Gosh, I love this cheesecake. The cheesecake is incredible on its own, but I find the garnishes make it phenomenal. There's a soft and crispy contrast between the cheesecake and the ginger snap cookie. There's also the sweet and spicy contrast of the pumpkin and ginger. For the finishing touch, a little apple balsamic vinegar brings it all together like a symphony on your palate.

Preheat the oven to 315°F.

Place a pot of hot water on the bottom rack of the oven. Add the cream cheese, sugars, and vanilla bean scrapings to a stand mixer with paddle attachment. Mix until a consistent creamy texture is formed, about 4 to 6 minutes. Once smooth, add the eggs one at a time. Add the next egg after the last is completely incorporated. After all the eggs are incorporated, fold in the pumpkin purée, cinnamon, nutmeg, cloves, and ginger. Mix until well combined, being sure to scrape the sides and bottom of the bowl for anything that may not have been pulled into the batter.

Increase the oven temperature to 325°F.

To make the Gingersnap Cookies: Add the butter, and sugars to a stand mixer with paddle attachment. Mix together on medium speed until combined. Add the fresh ginger, molasses, and vanilla. Mix until combined. Add the egg and continue to mix while being sure to scrape the sides and bottom of the bowl for anything that may not have been pulled into the batter. Add the baking soda, salt, ginger, cinnamon, cloves, and flour. Mix on low speed until combined. After a homogenous dough forms, remove the dough and place on a lightly floured surface.

Using a rolling pin, roll the dough to about ¼-inch thickness. Line a baking sheet with parchment paper. Cut the dough into 2-inch-wide

(Continued)

strips and as long as your baking sheet allows. Place the strips on the parchment paper and bake for 10 minutes. Turn the baking sheet and bake for another 6 minutes. Remove and allow to cool completely.

To make the Ginger Snap Crust: Place the baked cookies inside a food processor and pulse until the cookies turn into crumbs resembling coarse soil. Transfer the crumbs to a medium bowl and add the melted butter, brown sugar, and salt. Mix by hand until well combined. Note: The mixture should be able to hold itself together when a ball is packed tightly. More butter can be added if the mixture is a touch too dry. Once complete, pack the Ginger Snap Crust into the bottom of a 9 × 3-inch spring form cake pan. Bake for 12 minutes. Remove and cool for 10 minutes.

Once the crust is cooled, pour the cheesecake batter into the middle of the pan. Place in the oven and bake again for 1 hour 15 minutes. Remove from the oven and allow to cool completely before removing from the pan. Slice and drizzle a little apple balsamic vinegar on each piece to serve.

WINTER

Like many others, I find myself mostly indoors during the winter months compared to other times of the year. Because of that, I will spend more time at the kitchen table or in a cozy chair sipping a comforting cup of tea, hot chocolate, or a glass of bourbon. If you have a fireplace like BLACKBARN has in Saugerties, everything tastes better next to a crackling fire. There's definitely a shorter list of seasonal local produce to pick from, but that doesn't mean we have to eat the same dish every day, nor does it mean foods can't be exciting. At the restaurant, and at home, I will do more roasting and braising while the sauces get richer and ingredients like potatoes, gnocchi, and parsnips warm the soul. I find winter cooking brings out the richness in the ingredients we enjoy while garnishing with acidic foods such as grapes, apples, pomegranate seeds, vinegars, citrus and herbs creates a balance that elevates the meal and level of enjoyment.

GARDEN

ROASTED SWEET POTATO
WITH LENTILS AND ROASTED MUSHROOMS

SERVES 4 TO 6

SWEET POTATO
3 sweet potatoes, quartered
2 tablespoons Chipotle-
   Orange Spice Rub
   (page 134)

ROASTED MUSHROOMS
6 cups sliced, mixed, seasonal
   mushrooms (button,
   cremini, baby portobello,
   shiitake, oyster)
3 shallots, peeled and minced
4 sprigs fresh thyme
4 tablespoons olive oil
2 tablespoons sherry vinegar
2 tablespoons parsley,
   chopped
Sea salt, to taste

LABNEH
1 cup labneh or yogurt
1 tablespoon za'atar spice
3 tablespoons olive oil
1 teaspoon sea salt
⅛ teaspoon fresh cracked
   black pepper

LENTILS
¾ cup beluga lentils
¼ cup small-diced Spanish
   onion

Roasted sweet potato with lentils and roasted mushrooms is a hearty, nourishing dish perfect for any type of occasion. When I first ate this dish, it was love at first bite. The sweet potatoes, roasted until caramelized and tender, provide a subtle sweetness that contrasts beautifully with the earthy lentils. Roasted mushrooms add a rich, umami flavor, balancing the dish with their meaty texture. This combination is not only flavorful but also packed with nutrients, offering a great source of fiber, vitamins, and plant-based protein. It's a satisfying, wholesome meal that's easy to prepare and can be customized with herbs and spices to suit different tastes.

To make the Sweet Potatoes: Preheat the oven to 350°F. Season the sweet potatoes liberally with the Chipotle-Orange Spice Rub and place on a baking sheet. Place on the middle rack of the oven and bake for 24 minutes or until tender and golden brown. Set aside.

Increase the oven to 400°F.

To make the Roasted Mushrooms: Add the mushrooms, shallots, thyme, and olive oil to a large mixing bowl. Gently toss until combined and spread evenly on a sheet pan. Bake until the mushrooms are crispy on the edges, 30 to 40 minutes. Remove and drizzle with the sherry vinegar and season with parsley and salt. Set aside.

(Continued)

½ cup diced small carrots
2 sprigs fresh thyme
1 bay leaf
2½ cups Homemade
    Vegetable Stock
    (page 172)
¼ cup olive oil
½ tablespoon sea salt
¼ teaspoon fresh cracked
    black pepper

HERB VINAIGRETTE
MAKES 1½ CUPS
4 tablespoons chopped
    fresh mint
1 tablespoon chopped
    fresh dill
4 tablespoons chopped fresh
    Italian flat leaf parsley
½ tablespoon chopped fresh
    oregano
¼ cup red wine vinegar
¾ cup olive oil
½ teaspoon sugar
1½ teaspoons sea salt
¼ teaspoon fresh cracked
    black pepper

SALAD
5 cups mixed garden greens
Herb Vinaigrette

To make the Labneh: Add the labneh (or yogurt), za'atar spice, olive oil, salt, and pepper to a small mixing bowl. Mix until incorporated. Cover the bowl and place in the refrigerator until ready to serve.

To make the Lentils: Add the lentils, onions, carrots, thyme, bay leaf, and vegetable stock to a 4-quart saucepot over low heat. Cook until the lentils are tender, and the stock is fully absorbed, about 33 minutes. Season the pot with olive oil, salt, and pepper. Place in a warm place until ready to serve.

To make the Herb Vinaigrette: Add the mint, dill, parsley, oregano, vinegar, oil, sugar, salt and pepper to a medium-sized mixing bowl. Whisk vigorously until combined. Place in an airtight container and refrigerate until ready to use, for up to 2 days.

To serve, evenly distribute the Labneh on serving plates and spread with a spoon. Arrange the Sweet Potatoes, Lentils, and Roasted Mushrooms on the plate. Toss the mixed greens with the Herb Vinaigrette, add to the finished plates, and serve.

🍷 Wine Suggestion
Off-dry Riesling, Rheingau, Germany

CHESTNUT GNOCCHI
WITH BUTTER SAUCE AND MIXED WINTER VEGETABLES

SERVES 4 TO 6

CHESTNUT GNOCCHI
MAKES 9 CUPS FINISHED
GNOCCHI

2 pounds Idaho (Russet)
  potatoes, peeled

2 large eggs

3 egg yolks

4 tablespoons ricotta cheese

2 tablespoons mascarpone
  cheese

½ cup roasted chestnut
  powder

¾ cup "00" Italian superfine
  white flour

1 tablespoon kosher salt

⅛ teaspoon fresh cracked
  black pepper

BUTTER SAUCE
MAKES 1½ CUPS

1 cup heavy cream

10 tablespoons softened butter

Kosher salt and white pepper,
  to taste

MIXED WINTER VEGETABLES
MAKES 3 CUPS

½ pound Brussels sprouts,
  cleaned and halved
  lengthwise

½ pound turnips, cleaned and
  halved

4 cloves garlic, peeled and
  smashed

6 sprigs fresh thyme

4 tablespoons extra virgin
  olive oil

Kosher salt and fresh cracked
  black pepper, to taste

These little dumplings are the perfect use for chestnut flour. Slightly sweet and slightly nutty, these handcrafted gnocchi lend themselves very well to fall ingredients like mushrooms, grapes, pears, sage, acorn or butternut squash. Let this recipe and others be a guide, allowing you to get inspired and think creatively. In other words, think of the gnocchi as a blank canvas that you can have fun with and see where your culinary dreams take you.

To make the Potatoes: Bring a 4-quart stockpot with 4½ cups cold water to a boil over high heat. When boiling, add the potatoes and cook until fork tender, about 40 minutes. Remove the potatoes and pass them through a food mill or potato ricer into a large mixing bowl. While still warm, make a well in the center of the mound of potatoes. Let sit for 3 to 4 minutes to let some steam escape. Then pour the eggs and egg yolks into the well along with the ricotta and mascarpone.

Add the chestnut powder, flour, salt, and pepper to a mixing bowl and mix until well combined. Sprinkle around the perimeter of the potatoes. In the middle of the well, beat the eggs, ricotta, and mascarpone with a fork until combined.

With gentle hands, incorporate the potatoes into the egg mixture. As the potatoes and egg mixture become one, slowly incorporate the flour. The mixture will be very mealy and dry. Continue to knead the dough until it forms a soft ball. Be careful not to over-knead, as that will create dense gnocchi.

The finished dough should be smooth and light. If it is a bit too wet, add about one tablespoon of flour to the surface and gently pat it into the dough. Cover the dough with a damp kitchen towel and allow to rest for 10 minutes. This will allow the moisture in the potatoes to absorb the flour.

(Continued)

306 / BLACKBARN

GARNISH

2 Gala apples, julienned

¼ cup grated fresh Parmesan cheese

1 pomegranate, deseeded (1 pomegranate yields approximately 1½ cups of seeds)

Chipotle-Orange Spice Rub, to taste (page 134)

After 10 minutes, prepare to start rolling the dough. Place the dough on a work surface and slice off a piece about the size of an apple. With lightly floured hands, roll the dough into a rope about ¾-inch thick. Continue doing this until all the dough is rope shaped. Note: You can also place the ¾-inch pieces of dough on a sheet pan and freeze for later use. Ensure they are not touching before freezing. Then they can be transferred to a freezer bag.

Using a bench scraper or a knife, cut the rope into ¾-inch pieces. Sprinkle a touch of flour over them and gently toss, coating them evenly to avoid sticking. Once all the dough has been cut and tossed, place in the refrigerator until ready to cook.

This is a good time to prepare the Butter Sauce and roast the Mixed Winter Vegetables.

To make the Butter Sauce: Add the cream to a 1- or 2-quart saucepot over low-medium heat, and bring to a low simmer, while stirring occasionally. Reduce the cream by 20 percent without scorching the bottom of the pan, about 12 minutes. Once reduced, whisk in the butter until well combined. Season with salt and pepper and set aside until ready to use.

To make the Mixed Winter Vegetables: Preheat oven to 350°F. Add the Brussels sprouts, turnips, garlic, thyme, and olive oil to a large mixing bowl. Toss well and season with salt and pepper. Spread the vegetables evenly on a baking sheet lined with aluminum foil or parchment paper. Place on the middle rack in the oven and roast for 16 minutes, or until fork tender. Note: If your oven has a broil setting, place the cooked vegetables under the broiler for 2 minutes at the end to give them a light char and add another level of flavor.

To cook the gnocchi: Bring a large pot of salted water (about 10 cups of water with a pinch of salt) to a boil. Once boiling, carefully add the gnocchi in batches to avoid overcrowding and losing the boil. After about 30 seconds, the first gnocchi will begin to float. After floating, allow them to cook another 2 minutes or until all the gnocchi are floating. Using a spider or slotted spoon, transfer the gnocchi to a 9 × 13-inch casserole dish. Repeat this process until all of the gnocchi are cooked and in the dish. Pour the Butter Sauce over the gnocchi and mix gently.

Place the Mixed Winter Vegetables atop the gnocchi. Garnish with Gala apples, Parmesan, pomegranate seeds, and Chipotle-Orange Spice Rub to serve.

🍷 Wine Suggestion
Gewurztraminer, Grand Cru Alsace, France

OCEAN

THAI LOBSTER BISQUE EN CROÛTE

SERVES 8

4 (1¼-pound) live Maine
    lobsters
3 tablespoons olive oil, divided
½ cup brandy
1 cup lemongrass, sliced
2 cups fennel, sliced
2 cups peeled and sliced red
    onion
¾ cup peeled and minced
    ginger
2 tablespoons peeled and
    minced garlic
½ cup tomato paste
2 teaspoons red Thai curry
    paste
½ cup fresh lime juice
1½ quarts coconut milk
1½ quarts water
2 bay leaves
7 sprigs fresh thyme leaves
¼ teaspoon red pepper flakes
Sea salt and white pepper, to
    taste
6- to 8-inch round puff pastry
    circles, (store-bought)
Egg Wash (page 98)

If you're ready for a phenomenal flavor combination, try this sweet lobster and spicy Thai curry with lemongrass, ginger, and a touch of coconut milk which mellows out the dish. The aroma, taste, and visual of this dish is both mouthwatering and stunning. At my home, it's a crowd pleaser every time. In fact, my son Patrick told me it was the best dish he's ever tasted and always asks for it whenever he comes to BLACKBARN.

Bring a salted pot of water to a boil over high heat. Once boiling, add the lobsters and cook for 3 to 4 minutes. Remove and immediately transfer to an ice bath then remove the meat from the tail and claws and set aside.

Dice the lobster meat into ½-inch pieces. Place all the meat on a plate, cover with plastic wrap, and refrigerate until ready to use. Reserve all the shells.

To make the Soup: Add 2 tablespoons of oil to an 8- to 12-quart pot over high heat. Heat the oil until shimmering. Add the lobster shells and cook until bright red, 8 to 10 minutes. Remove the shells from the pot and reserve them in a bowl. Reduce the heat to medium and add the brandy, scraping the bottom of the pot with a wooden spoon. Pour the brandy into the bowl of lobster shells. Add the remaining tablespoon of oil to the pot and increase the heat back to high. When the oil is shimmering, add the lemongrass, fennel, and onions and cook

(Continued)

until wilted, about 8 minutes. Add the ginger and garlic and continue cooking for 3 minutes. Add the tomato paste and curry paste and cook for 2 minutes. Add the lime juice, coconut milk, water, bay leaves, thyme, red pepper flakes, and the reserved lobster shells with brandy. Mix all ingredients until the liquid boils, then reduce the heat to a simmer. Allow to simmer for 1 hour. Strain and adjust the seasoning with salt and white pepper.

Distribute the reserved lobster meat into 6 to 8 (8- to 10-ounce) oven-safe casserole dishes. Top with the soup, leaving about ½ inch at the top.

Lightly egg-wash the rim of each dish and lay one puff pastry sheet over the dish. Gently mold the edges of the pastry sheet around the rim of the dish to ensure the dough stays in place. Egg wash the top of the puff pastry and place in the refrigerator for 30 minutes.

Preheat the oven to 375°F.

Bake for 25 minutes and serve.

HOLIDAY PARTIES

Holiday meals have a way of bringing people together. The table fills with conversation, glasses are raised, and plates are passed around. Whether it's a yearly tradition, or a chance to reconnect, these moments remind us what the season is all about—good food, great company, and time well spent.

OLIVE OIL BRAISED OCTOPUS

WITH HUMMUS AND PRESERVED LEMON GREMOLATA

SERVES 4 TO 8

1 (4- to 6-pound) octopus
2 cups red wine
½ large Spanish onion, peeled and large diced
4 cloves garlic, smashed
1 jalapeño, cut in half lengthwise
1 bunch fresh thyme
6 bay leaves
2 lemons, halved
1 carrot, large diced
2 red bell peppers, large diced
8 traditional wine corks, optional
4 cups + ¼ cup olive oil, divided
Coarse sea salt, to taste

PRESERVED LEMON GREMOLATA
MAKES 2 CUPS

⅔ cup olive oil for cooking, plus ½ cup for finishing
3 tablespoons chopped garlic
3 tablespoons pine nuts
4 tablespoons diced preserved lemons
1 cup diced pitted Queen olives
½ cup diced capers
5 tablespoons diced shallots
6 tablespoons chopped fresh Italian flat leaf parsley
2 tablespoons chopped fresh thyme

This recipe has been on our menu since day one. The typical feedback I get from guests is, "This is the best octopus I've ever had," so it remains on the menu. The braising part can be done days ahead of time and then either grill or pan-sear when it's time to eat. The texture is tender with just the right amount of chewiness, and the hummus, salad, and lemon-olive gremolata bring all the right flavors and textures together.

To make the Octopus: Preheat the oven to 325°F. Bring an 8-quart pot of water to boil. With a set of tongs, blanch the octopus by submerging it in the boiling water for 15 seconds and removing it for 10 to 15 seconds. Repeat this four times. Discard the water, and then return the blanched octopus to the pot. Add the red wine, onion, garlic, jalapeño, thyme, bay leaves, lemons, carrot, bell peppers, wine corks, 4 cups of olive oil, and sea salt. Bring it to a boil, and then lower the temperature to a gentle simmer for 2½ hours. Remove the octopus and allow it to cool. While the octopus is simmering, prepare the Hummus and the Preserved Lemon Gremolata.

To make the Preserved Lemon Gremolata: Add the ⅔ cup olive oil and garlic to a 10-inch sauté pan over medium heat. Using a rubber spatula or wooden spoon, gently move the garlic so it does not stick to the bottom of the pan. Continue to cook until the garlic is fragrant and turns golden brown, about 6 minutes. Add the pine nuts, preserved lemons, olives, and capers and stir to combine. Turn off the heat and immediately add the shallots. The residual heat from the pan will soften the shallots perfectly. Add the parsley and thyme, mix well, and let cool. Transfer to an airtight container with the remaining ½ cup olive oil. Keep at room temperature until ready to serve or refrigerate for up to 2 weeks.

(Continued)

ROASTED GARLIC CLOVES

2 large garlic bulbs, cut in half lengthwise
4 tablespoons extra virgin olive oil, plus more for preserving
Sea salt, to taste

HUMMUS
MAKES 3 CUPS

2 cups canned chickpeas, drained
2 roasted red peppers (canned or freshly prepared)
½ cup tahini paste
1 tablespoon sesame oil
2 Roasted Garlic Cloves
3 tablespoons fresh lime juice
½ cup olive oil
Kosher salt and fresh cracked black pepper, to taste

To make the Roasted Garlic Cloves: Preheat the oven to 350°F. Place the garlic heads in aluminum foil and drizzle the cut side with the olive oil. Season with salt and wrap the garlic tightly. Poke a little hole on top so steam can escape. Place the wrapped garlic on a baking sheet and on the middle rack of the oven. Bake until the garlic is deep golden brown and tender, about 45 minutes. Remove and let cool for 20 minutes. Using a rubber spatula, scoop the roasted garlic out of its skin. Set aside until ready to use. The remaining garlic can be stored in an airtight container in the refrigerator submerged in olive oil for up to 2 weeks.

To make the Hummus: Add the chickpeas, red peppers, tahini, sesame oil, Roasted Garlic Cloves, lime juice, and olive oil to a food processor and blend until smooth. Season to taste with salt and pepper. Transfer to an airtight container and refrigerate until ready to use, for up to 1 week.

Once the octopus has fully cooled, slice off each tentacle and discard the head. Coat a skillet using the remaining olive oil over medium-high heat. Add enough tentacles to cover the bottom of the pan and brown them evenly. Repeat until all of the tentacles are crisp. Spread the Hummus evenly on individual serving plates, followed by 1 or 2 tentacles. Finish by drizzling the Preserved Lemon Gremolata over the top and serve.

HERB-CRUSTED ATLANTIC COD

WITH SEASONAL MUSHROOMS AND PARSLEY SAUCE

SERVES 6

HERB CRUST AND COD

3 tablespoons olive oil, divided
1 tablespoon minced shallots
½ teaspoon minced garlic
1 cup Italian flat leaf parsley
2 tablespoons fresh tarragon
1 tablespoon fresh thyme
    leaves
¼ cup sliced fresh chives
½ teaspoon lemon zest
¾ cup Japanese breadcrumbs
Sea salt and white pepper,
    to taste
6 (5-ounce) fresh cod filets

PARSLEY SAUCE
MAKES 2 CUPS

1 bunch fresh Italian flat leaf
    parsley, cleaned and rinsed
2 large russet potatoes,
    peeled and large diced
1 quart Homemade Vegetable
    Stock (page 172)
Kosher salt and fresh cracked
    black pepper, to taste
¼ cup olive oil

SEASONAL MUSHROOMS
MAKES ABOUT 1½ CUPS

3 tablespoons olive oil
½ pound seasonal mushrooms,
    cleaned and cut into
    evenly sized pieces
2 shallots, peeled and minced
3 fresh thyme sprigs
⅛ cup sherry vinegar
Kosher salt and fresh cracked
    black pepper, to taste

I find cod to be a delicious and versatile fish. Cod is also very affordable and contains enough fat to keep the fish moist while the flesh itself offers a pleasant, flaky texture with enough flavor to stand up to strong ingredients. You'll discover that preparing and cooking the cod is quite simple. If you ever find yourself with halibut on hand, it works well here too.

To make the Herb Crust: Add 2 tablespoons of oil to a skillet over high heat. When heated and the oil is shimmering, add the shallots and garlic. Reduce the heat to medium and cook until the shallots and garlic are translucent, about 4 minutes. Once cooked, remove and transfer to a food processor along with the parsley, tarragon, thyme, chives, and lemon zest. Mix well and add the breadcrumbs, season with salt and white pepper and mix again until thoroughly combined. Refrigerate until ready to use.

To make the Cod: Coat the cod filets with the olive oil, and season with the salt and white pepper. Space the filets out on a sheet pan. Evenly distribute the herb breadcrumbs on top of each filet, creating a top coating about ¼-inch thick. Place the sheet pan in the oven for 12 to 15 minutes. Cooking times will vary depending on the thickness of the fish. Remove when the fish feels firm when squeezed from the sides.

To make the Parsley Sauce: Prepare an ice bath (bowl of ice and water used to quickly cool ingredients, halt cooking, and preserve color and texture) and set aside. Fill a 2-quart saucepot halfway with water, place over high heat, and bring to a boil. When boiling, add the parsley and boil for 20 seconds. Remove the parsley and immediately place in the ice water bath to stop the cooking process. Empty the pot and add the potatoes and vegetable stock. Season with salt and pepper. Return to high heat and bring to a boil. Once boiling, reduce the heat to a low

(Continued)

simmer. Cook until the potatoes are fork tender, about 12 to 14 minutes. Strain the potatoes and transfer to a blender, reserving the liquid. Blend using the reserved liquid to adjust the thickness. Blend until the potatoes reach a smooth consistency. While still blending, drizzle in the oil, followed by the blanched parsley. Transfer to a container until ready to serve, or store in an airtight container in the refrigerator for up to 1 week.

To make the Seasonal Mushrooms: Add the olive oil to a 10-inch sauté pan over medium-high heat. When the oil is heated and shimmering, add the shallots and thyme and sauté until the shallots are translucent, about 4 to 6 minutes. Add the mushrooms and continue to sauté until all their water has been released. Add the sherry vinegar and cook until nearly dry. Season to taste and set aside to cool.

Spoon and spread about 2 tablespoons of Parsley Sauce on the serving plates, followed by a cod filet. Garnish with the Seasonal Mushrooms and serve.

🍷 Wine Suggestion
Semillon - Sauvignon Blanc blend, Boudreaux Blanc, France

BEAVER KILL TROUT
WITH BROCCOLI, HEIRLOOM CARROTS, SHAVED FINGERLINGS, AND POMEGRANATE-BLOOD ORANGE

SERVES 4

TROUT

4 tablespoons olive oil + more for drizzling

3 tablespoons fresh lemon juice

1 teaspoon smoked paprika

¼ cup chopped fresh dill

2 whole trout, cleaned and deboned with head on

Kosher salt and fresh cracked black pepper, to taste

2 cups thinly shaved fingerling potatoes

2 cups thinly shaved tri-colored heirloom carrots

2 cups thinly shaved broccoli florets

GARNISH

1 fresh pomegranate, seeded

2 blood oranges, cut into supremes

2 teaspoons olive oil

3 tablespoons fresh Italian flat leaf parsley, leaves only

What's so special about this dish, aside from how delicious it is, is how easy the trout is to make. A few simple knife cuts and some beautiful locally sourced fish, and you have a great one-pan dinner! Whether it's for yourself or feeding a large group, this flavor-packed trout is sure to get some attention around the dinner table.

Preheat the oven 350°F.

To make the Trout: Add the 4 tablespoons olive oil along with the lemon juice, smoked paprika, and dill to a small bowl. Mix to combine, then spoon the mixture all over the exterior of the trout. Season with salt and pepper. From head to tail, on both sides, make 1-inch cuts into the skin-side of each trout (about 4 or 5 cuts on each side). Layer the shaved potatoes on a greased baking pan, followed by the carrots and broccoli. Season with salt pepper and a drizzle of olive oil. Place the trout, closed, on top of the vegetables. Bake for 20 minutes. Gently remove the trout so it doesn't fall apart and set aside. Return the baking sheet to the oven and cook for another 15 minutes, or until the vegetables are tender and evenly browed.

To make the Garnish: Add the pomegranate seeds, oranges, olive oil, and parsley leaves to a small bowl. Mix to combine and set aside.

To assemble, spoon the vegetable mixture in the center of each plate. Place a trout on top. Top with pomegranate–blood orange garnish and serve.

🍷 Wine Suggestion
Sauvignon Blanc, Sancerre, France

A NOTE ABOUT TROUT

When purchasing trout at the market, several factors ensure you get the best quality. First, check for freshness by examining the fish's eyes; they should be clear and not sunken. The flesh should be firm and bounce back when touched, and it should have a mild, fresh scent rather than a strong, fishy odor. The gills should be bright red or pink, indicating freshness, and the skin should be shiny and moist.

If buying whole trout, ensure the scales are intact and not dull or dry. For filets, look for a clean, translucent appearance without any browning or discoloration. It's also important to buy from a reputable fishmonger or market where you can inquire about the source of the trout, whether it's farmed or wild, as this can affect flavor and sustainability.

Consider the fish's intended use; wild trout (particularly rainbow, brown, and brook) often has a richer flavor, while farmed trout may have a milder taste and more consistent texture. Proper storage is crucial, so keep trout chilled and use it within a day or two for the best quality.

PASTURE

SEARED VENISON CHOP AND RAVIOLO
WITH CELERY ROOT-APPLE PURÉE

SERVES 5 TO 7

VENISON

1 rack of venison, cut into 5 to 7 chops (some chops will have 2 bones)
4 cloves garlic, peeled and smashed
3 sprigs fresh thyme leaves
1 tablespoon ground nutmeg
7 tablespoons olive oil
Kosher salt to taste
Fresh cracked black pepper, to taste

BRAISED VENISON SHOULDER

4 tablespoons olive oil
1½ pounds venison shoulder, large diced
Kosher salt, to taste
1 large carrot, large diced
1 Spanish onion, peeled and large diced
3 cloves garlic, peeled and smashed
1 tablespoon all-purpose flour
1 sprig rosemary, minced
10 sage leaves, minced
2 bay leaves
¼ cup raisins

Cooking the same meat two ways and serving them together is something we often do with pork, lamb, wild boar, and poultry. On every animal, there are tender cuts that eat well (like the loin) but have less moisture and flavor. Then there are the tougher muscles, which are used more by the animal and retain a lot more flavor. To get a tough cut tender, the meat must be braised or slow roasted for a long period while the loin is quickly grilled or sautéed. This fantastic dish features both delicious cuts.

To marinate the Venison: Coat the venison chops with the garlic, thyme, nutmeg, and olive oil, and set them aside until it is time to cook them.

To make the Braised Venison Shoulder: Add the oil to a 3-quart saucepot over low-medium heat. When the oil is heated and shimmering, add the diced venison, season with salt, and brown on all sides. Use a slotted spoon to remove and reserve the meat. Add the carrot, onion, and garlic. Cook for 3 to 4 minutes. Add the flour and stir. Add the venison, rosemary, sage, bay leaves, raisins, red wine, and bone broth. Cook on a low simmer for 2½ to 3 hours, or until venison is fork tender. Remove the bay leaves and set aside to cool.

To make the Celery Root and Apple Puree: Add the celery root, potatoes, apples, milk, cream, vanilla pod and seeds, onion, and thyme

(Continued)

2 cups red wine
1½ cups bone broth

CELERY ROOT–APPLE PURÉE
MAKES 2 CUPS
½ celery root, large diced
1 russet potato, peeled
1 Granny Smith apple
2 cups whole milk
1 cup heavy cream
½ vanilla bean, split and
    scraped
1 Spanish onion, peeled and
    medium diced
12 sprigs fresh thyme, tied
    into a herb bouquet

PASTA DOUGH
4 cups "00" flour
¼ cup semolina flour + more
    for dusting
4 large eggs
6 egg yolks Egg Wash
    (page 98)

bouquet to a 4-quart pot over medium heat. Simmer until the celery root and potatoes are fork tender, about 12 to 14 minutes. Once cooked, discard the vanilla bean pod, transfer the solid ingredients to a blender and blend on high, using the cooking liquid to control the consistency. When finished, the purée should resemble a creamy paste. Set aside until ready to use or store in an airtight container for up to 1 week.

To make the Pasta Dough: Add the "00" flour, ¼ cup semolina, eggs, and yolks to a stand mixer with the dough hook attachment. Mix until a homogenous dough has formed. Pull the dough from the bowl and place on a floured surface. Cover with a damp towel and allow to rest for 30 minutes.

Separate the dough into two even portions and keep one covered. With a rolling pin, roll the uncovered dough into a rectangular shape. Pass the pasta dough through a pasta dough sheeter on the widest setting. After each pass, gradually lower the gauge and continue until reaching the second lowest setting. Then, cut the dough into 15 × 6-inch sheets (the smaller side will depend on the pasta sheeter used). Repeat this step 4 times.

Pack the reserved Braised Venison Shoulder into a ¼ cup and turn out onto the dough, 2-inches apart. Brush the Egg Wash onto the pasta dough around the edge of the venison 1-inch in diameter. Lay a fresh sheet of pasta dough loosely over the venison. Gently cup your hands (one in the shape of a C and the others a backwards C) around the venison, binding the layers together. Repeat until all the venison has been covered with the new sheets. Using either a ring mold or a pizza cutter, cut the dough around the ravioli, leaving about ½-inch of the pasta from the edge to where the dough has been filled with the venison. Sprinkle the ravioli lightly with semolina and set aside until ready to cook. You can also refrigerate the ravioli, covered with a dry towel, for up to 2 days.

To cook the ravioli, add them to a pot of boiling water for 8 to 10 minutes. If the ravioli were previously refrigerated, boil for 13 to 15 minutes and set aside.

Preheat the oven to 385°F.

To finish the venison chops: Season the marinated chops with salt and pepper. Add the remaining 4 tablespoons of oil to a 10-inch oven-safe skillet over high heat. Once the oil is shimmering, add the venison chops, flesh side down. Reduce the heat to medium-high and sear for 4 minutes on each side. Place the skillet in the oven for 6 minutes for medium rare (130°F). Remove and allow to rest for 5 minutes before serving with the Ravioli.

🍷 Wine Suggestion
Nebbiolo, Barolo, Piedmont, Italy

MILK BRAISED OSSOBUCO

WITH CREAMY POLENTA AND ROASTED MUSHROOMS

SERVES 4

OSSOBUCO
½ cup cubbed pancetta
½ cup diced carrot
½ cup diced celery
1 cup diced yellow onion
4 cloves garlic, chopped
2 sprigs fresh rosemary, finely chopped
4 sprigs fresh thyme, finely chopped
½ cup tomato purée
Kosher salt and fresh cracked black pepper, to taste
2½- to 3½ pounds veal shanks, cut into 4 (2½-inch thick) portions
½ cup flour for dusting
2 bay leaves
2 cups whole milk
2 cups white wine
Chopped fresh Italian flat leaf parsley, for garnish
Freshly grated Parmesan cheese, for garnish
4 cups Sautéed Mixed Seasonal Roasted Mushrooms (page 302)

CREAMY POLENTA
3 cups whole milk
Kosher salt and fresh cracked black pepper, to taste
1 cup coarse polenta
4 tablespoons unsalted butter
1 cup Parmesan cheese

Milk-braised ossobuco with creamy polenta and roasted mushrooms is an indulgent, flavorful dish that brings together tender meat, rich textures, and comforting flavors. Ossobuco, typically a slow-braised veal shank, becomes incredibly tender when braised in milk, which imparts a delicate, creamy flavor to the meat while balancing its richness. The braising process also creates a silky sauce perfect for pairing with creamy polenta. I find the polenta serves as a soft, comforting base, absorbing the sauce and enhancing the overall depth of flavor. Meanwhile, the roasted mushrooms complement this dish with their earthy, umami taste, adding a slight bite that contrasts with the softness of the polenta and meat. Together, these components create a harmonious, well-rounded meal that feels both rustic and sophisticated. It's an ideal dish for special occasions or when you want to treat yourself to a luxurious, comforting dinner.

Add the carrot, celery, onion, and garlic to a food processor. Mix until finely minced. Transfer to a medium sized bowl and add the rosemary, thyme, tomato purée, salt, and pepper. Mix well and set aside.

Preheat the oven to 325°F. Season the veal with salt and pepper. Dredge in flour and set aside.

In a Dutch oven over medium heat, cook the pancetta until brown. Remove and reserve. Using the liquefied fat from the pancetta, add the seasoned veal and brown on both sides.

Once the veal has seared on both sides, remove from the pan and set aside. Add the reserved vegetable mixture and the bay leaves to the Dutch oven, and cook for 5 minutes. Using a wooden spoon, scrape the bottom and sides of the pan. Add the veal back along with the milk and wine and stir. Bring to a boil then reduce the heat and let simmer. Check

(Continued)

for seasoning and continue cooking covered in the oven for about 2 to 2½ hours or until fork tender.

Make the Roasted Mushrooms (page 302) and set aside.

To make the Creamy Polenta: Add the milk, 3 cups water, salt, and pepper to a 4-quart saucepot over high heat. Bring to a simmer. Once simmering, whisk in the polenta and continue whisking until the polenta starts absorbing the milk and water. The mixture should start to thicken slightly. Reduce the heat and cover with a lid. Allow to cook for 25 minutes. Note: Use a wooden spoon to stir during the cooking process as the polenta will naturally stick to the bottom of the pot. Remove from the heat, add the butter and cheese, and set aside.

To plate, place the Creamy Polenta in the center of individual serving plates. Add the ossobuco on top, followed by the Roasted Mushrooms. Garnish with parsley and Parmesan and serve.

🍷 Wine Suggestion
Pinot Noir, Premier Cru Burgundy, France

SIDES

ROASTED BRUSSELS SPROUTS

SERVES 4 TO 6

1½ pounds Brussels sprouts, halved
2 Gala apples, diced
½ pound bacon, cut into ¼-inch-thick pieces
6 sprigs fresh thyme leaves
8 cloves garlic, smashed
6 tablespoons olive oil
Kosher salt and fresh cracked black pepper, to taste

These Roasted Brussels Sprouts with diced apple, bacon, thyme, and garlic are a deliciously savory-sweet side dish we serve often at BLACKBARN. The crispy Brussels sprouts, caramelized in the oven, pair beautifully with smoky bacon and the subtle sweetness of diced apples while the fresh thyme adds an earthy aroma, and the garlic infuses the dish with a robust depth of flavor. This combination of textures and tastes creates a well-balanced, flavorful accompaniment perfect for winter meals or holiday gatherings.

Preheat the oven to 385°F.

Add the Brussels sprouts, apples, bacon, thyme, and garlic to a medium-sized bowl. Toss with the olive oil and season with salt and pepper. Arrange on a lined baking sheet and roast in the middle rack of the oven for 14 minutes. Remove from oven and serve.

BLACK WINTER TRUFFLE GNOCCHI

SERVES 4 TO 6

RICOTTA GNOCCHI
1¼ cups ricotta cheese
1¾ cups freshly grated
   Parmesan cheese, divided
¾ cup "00" flour
2 large eggs
Kosher salt, to taste
2½ cups Butter Sauce

TRUFFLE BUTTER SAUCE
MAKES 2½ CUPS
3 cups heavy cream
¼ cup chopped black winter
   truffle
¾ cup cold diced unsalted
   butter
¼ cup black winter truffle,
   grated, for garnish
1 cup Parmesan, for garnish
Kosher salt and white pepper,
   to taste

Black Winter Truffle Gnocchi is a luxurious and indulgent dish that highlights the rich, earthy aroma of truffles. The delicate, pillowy gnocchi absorbs the simple yet decadent butter sauce, allowing the black winter truffle's deep, musky flavor to shine. Finished with Parmesan, this dish is an elegant balance of textures and flavors, making it perfect for special occasions or when you're craving something refined yet comforting.

To make the Gnocchi: Add the ricotta, 1¼ cups Parmesan, flour, eggs, and salt to a stand mixer with the paddle attachment. Mix on low speed until a homogenous dough forms. Transfer the dough to a lightly floured work surface.

Cover the dough with a damp kitchen towel and let rest for 10 minutes. Then, place the dough on a work surface and slice off a piece about the size of an apple. With lightly floured hands, roll the dough into a rope about ¾-inches thick. Continue until all the dough is rope shaped.

Using a bench scraper or knife, cut the rope into ¾-inch pieces. Sprinkle a touch of flour over them and gently toss through the flour, coating evenly to avoid sticking. Once all the dough has been cut and tossed, refrigerate until ready to cook.

To make the Butter Sauce: Add the heavy cream and truffles to a 3-quart saucepot over medium-high heat. Bring to a boil then lower to a simmer and reduce by one third. Once reduced, whisk in the butter. Continue whisking until the butter has completely melted and the sauce coats the back of a spoon. Whisk in the Parmesan cheese. Season to taste with salt and pepper then remove from heat and set aside.

(Continued)

To Cook the Gnocchi: Bring a large pot of salted water to a boil. Once boiling, carefully drop the gnocchi into the water in batches to avoid overcrowding and losing the boil. After about 30 seconds, the first gnocchi will begin to float. After floating, allow the gnocchi to cook another 2 minutes or until all the gnocchi are floating. Using a spider or slotted spoon, transfer the gnocchi to a 9 × 13-inch casserole dish. Pour the Truffle Butter Sauce over the gnocchi, gently toss, then garnish with shaved truffle before serving.

DESSERT

RUM BUTTERSCOTCH BREAD PUDDING

SERVES 6

**VANILLA BEAN ICE CREAM
MAKES 8 CUPS**
1 cup egg yolks
1½ cups sugar
4 cups whole milk
1 teaspoon sea salt
2 vanilla beans, split and scraped
2 cups heavy cream

CUSTARD
6 eggs
¾ cup dark brown sugar
2 cups whole milk
2½ cups heavy cream
1 teaspoon vanilla extract
½ teaspoon salt
6 tablespoons dark rum

BREAD
1½ pound loaf brioche, cut
    into 1-inch squares
5 tablespoons butterscotch
    chips
6 tablespoons golden raisins

TOFFEE SAUCE
1 cup brown sugar
¼ cup water
3 tablespoons diced unsalted
    butter
3 tablespoons molasses
1½ cups heavy cream

When we first opened BLACKBARN, our bread pudding was only available in our Tavern, where the menu is more casual with homestyle items. It didn't feel right to have such a simple dessert on our Main Dining Room dessert menu next to our other more refined and artistic offerings. It wasn't long before our servers started asking, if not insisting, that the bread pudding be included based on raves from our Tavern guests. Reluctantly, but not regrettably, I gave in. Today, our bread pudding and Apple Cider Doughnuts (page 292) are two dessert staples I have come to identify as authentic and approachable, and which you'll find in our Main Dining Room.

To make the Vanilla Bean Ice Cream: Add the egg yolks and sugar to a stand mixer with whisk attachment and mix on medium speed until thick and pale yellow, about 4 to 5 minutes. Meanwhile, add the milk, salt, and vanilla bean (with pods) to a saucepot over low heat. Bring to a simmer then, with a stand mixer on low speed, gradually pour the scalding milk-vanilla mixture into the egg yolk and sugar mixture. Allow to temper for 5 minutes on low speed. Remove and transfer the mixture to a bowl and heat over a bain-marie or hot water bath, stirring continuously, until the mixture coats the back of a spoon. Stir in the heavy cream and immediately place the bowl in a cold-water bath to quickly cool. Once cool, freeze in an ice cream maker according to the manufacturer's instructions.

(Continued)

To make the Custard: Add the eggs, brown sugar, milk, heavy cream, vanilla, salt, and dark rum to a medium-sized mixing bowl. Mix to combine then refrigerate until ready to use.

Preheat the oven to 315°F.

To make the Bread Pudding: Add the diced brioche to a sheet pan and place in the oven until toasted, about 10 to 12 minutes. Remove and let cool. Transfer the cool toasted brioche to either 6 individual baking dishes or a 9 × 13-inch oven-safe casserole dish, ensuring the brioche is arranged in a single layer. Evenly distribute the butterscotch chips and raisins. Pour the custard over the brioche until nearly covered, and let sit for 20 minutes, allowing the custard to soak into the bread.

Raise the oven to 325°F.

Bake for 25 minutes or until the center is firm to the touch.

To make the Toffee Sauce: Add the brown sugar and ¼ cup water to a 2-quart saucepot over medium-high heat. Stir to combine and bring to a boil. Cook 7 minutes. Note: A good way to tell how caramelized the sugars are, is by paying close attention to the size of the bubbles in the pot. When first coming to a boil, the bubbles will be large. When the syrup begins to enter the soft-crack stage, the bubbles will become smaller and closer together. At this point, the moisture or water in the recipe has evaporated and the sugars are caramelizing. Remove the pot from the heat and gradually add the butter and molasses. Whisk the butter and the molasses into the caramel until the butter has melted and the caramel begins to look silky, about 6 to 8 minutes. Return to medium-low heat. Whisk in the heavy cream and lightly simmer until the mixture thickens, 12 to 15 minutes. Remove from the heat and set aside.

Remove the casserole from the oven, drizzle the Toffee Sauce over the top, add a scoop or two of Vanilla Bean Ice Cream, and serve.

FROSTED ROOT CARROT CAKE

WITH BLOOD ORANGE CREAM CHEESE

MAKES 1 (9-INCH) CAKE

FROSTED ROOT CARROT CAKE

1 cup vegetable oil
1 cup whole eggs
2 cups sugar
1 teaspoon vanilla extract
1¾ cups all-purpose flour
1 teaspoon baking powder
½ teaspoon baking soda
½ teaspoon kosher salt
½ teaspoon cinnamon
¼ teaspoon ground nutmeg
¼ teaspoon ground cloves
4 cups loosely packed shredded carrots
Toasted pistachios, as needed, for garnish, optional

BLOOD ORANGE CREAM CHEESE

1 cup cream cheese, softened
½ cup powdered sugar
1 blood orange, zested
3 tablespoons blood orange juice
2 drops orange food coloring, optional
1 cup heavy whipping cream

Carrot cake is such an American classic and a perfect fit for our farm to table concept. Pastry Chef Kerry has developed the perfect carrot cake with the addition of blood orange and pistachios. We've gotten more compliments on this dessert than any other. I think this dessert truly represents Kerry as an innovative pastry chef.

To make the Frosted Root Carrot Cake: Preheat the oven to 350°F. Add the vegetable oil, eggs, sugar, and vanilla to a stand mixer with whisk attachment. Whisk on medium speed for 10 minutes, or until pale and fluffy. While the wet ingredients are whisking, sift the flour, baking powder, baking soda, salt, cinnamon, nutmeg, and cloves together in a mixing bowl. Then add the "dry" ingredients to the "wet" ingredients and whisk until combined. Fold in the shredded carrots. Spray a 9-inch cake pan and pour the cake batter inside. Bake for 10 minutes, rotate, and bake for another 10 minutes. Check for doneness by poking the top of the cake with a finger. If it springs back, the cake is done. Once done, remove and let cool.

To make the Blood Orange Cream Cheese: Add the cream cheese and powdered sugar to a large mixing bowl. Mix until combined and no lumps are visible. Add the orange zest, blood orange juice, and food coloring, if using. Mix again until combined. Transfer the cream cheese mixture to another large bowl and set aside. Add the heavy cream to a stand mixer with whisk attachment and whip on high speed until stiff peaks form. Remove and fold the whipped cream into the cream cheese mixture.

Spread the Blood Orange Cream Cheese on top of the carrot cake. Sprinkle with toasted pistachios, if desired, and serve.

ACKNOWLEDGMENTS

The BLACKBARN authors would like to give special thanks to all those who assisted and supported with the making of this book. In no particular order, we would like to thank:

Erin Hayes, Chefs Brian Fowler, Marcos Castro, Kerry Hegarty, and our entire BLACKBARN Restaurant team.

To the cookbook production team, particularly James O. Fraioli and Culinary Book Creations, Alan Hebel and Ian Koviak of The Book Designers. Editor Varsana Tikovsky. Senior Editors Nicole Frail and Jesse McHugh, and the teams at Skyhorse Publishing and Simon & Schuster.

Photographers Alan Batt (Battman Studios), Mark Zhelezoglo, Dillon Burke, Andrija Tadejevic, and Melisa Hom.

To all our farmers, ranchers, fisherman, and cheesemakers.

Thank you.

METRIC CONVERSIONS

If you're accustomed to using metric measurements, use these handy charts to convert the imperial measurements used in this book.

Weight (Dry Ingredients)

1 oz		30 g
4 oz	$\frac{1}{4}$ lb	120 g
8 oz	$\frac{1}{2}$ lb	240 g
12 oz	$\frac{3}{4}$ lb	360 g
16 oz	1 lb	480 g
32 oz	2 lb	960 g

Volume (Liquid Ingredients)

$\frac{1}{2}$ tsp.		2 ml
1 tsp.		5 ml
1 Tbsp.	$\frac{1}{2}$ fl oz	15 ml
2 Tbsp.	1 fl oz	30 ml
$\frac{1}{4}$ cup	2 fl oz	60 ml
$\frac{1}{3}$ cup	3 fl oz	80 ml
$\frac{1}{2}$ cup	4 fl oz	120 ml
$\frac{2}{3}$ cup	5 fl oz	160 ml
$\frac{3}{4}$ cup	6 fl oz	180 ml
1 cup	8 fl oz	240 ml
1 pt	16 fl oz	480 ml
1 qt	32 fl oz	960 ml

Oven Temperatures

Fahrenheit	Celsius	Gas Mark
225°	110°	$\frac{1}{4}$
250°	120°	$\frac{1}{2}$
275°	140°	1
300°	150°	2
325°	160°	3
350°	180°	4
375°	190°	5
400°	200°	6
425°	220°	7
450°	230°	8

Length

$\frac{1}{4}$ in	6 mm
$\frac{1}{2}$ in	13 mm
$\frac{3}{4}$ in	19 mm
1 in	25 mm
6 in	15 cm
12 in	30 cm

INDEX

A

aioli
    Maine Lobster Roll, 116–118
ale
    Belgian
        IPA Braised Cheshire Pork Shank,
            198–200
allspice
    Homemade Hot Sauce, 92
Almond Honey Croissant, 96–98
almonds
    Chorizo Egg and Cheese Empanada,
        130–132
    Roasted Peaches, 245
anchovy fillets
    Charred Gem Lettuce, 112
apple cider
    Roasted Acorn Squash, 290
Apple Cider Doughnuts, 292–294
apples
    Almond Honey Croissant, 96–98
    Gala
        Chestnut Gnocchi, 306–309
        Corn Flake Crusted French Toast,
            122
        Roasted Acorn Squash, 290
        Roasted Brussels Sprouts, 334
    Granny Smith
        Apple Cider Doughnuts, 292–
            294
        Seared Venison Chop and
            Raviolo, 326–329
    green
        Green Juice, 84
arugula
    Black Mission Fig Pizza, 256–258
asparagus
    Crab Cakes with Spinach-Ramp
        Purée, 184–186
    white
        White Asparagus with Morel
            Mushrooms and Buttermilk
            Dressing, 172–174
avocado
    Bigeye Tuna Tartare, 220–222
    Charred Gem Lettuce, 112
Avocado Toast, 108

B

bacon
    BLACKBARN Burger, 134–136
    Butternut Squash Ravioli, 268–270

Grilled Corn and Kale Salad,
    214–216
Roasted Brussels Sprouts, 334
Barbecue Sauce, 138
    BLACKBARN Burger, 134–136
    Crispy Chicken Wings, 162
    Eight-Hour Barbecue Beef Ribs,
        282
Barnyard Tea, 150
basil
    BLACKBARN Burger, 134–136
    Blushing Basil, 152
    Bone Marrow with Manila Clams
        and Shallot Reduction, 192–194
    Maine Lobster Roll, 116–118
    Polenta Cake with Ratatouille and
        Marinated Shrimp, 230–232
    Ricotta Zeppole, 176–178
bay leaves
    Bone Marrow with Manila Clams
        and Shallot Reduction, 192–194
    Butter Poached Maine Lobster with
        Fresh Pea Soup, 224
    Crab Cakes with Spinach-Ramp
        Purée, 184–186
    Crisp-Skinned Striped Bass,
        274–276
    Cuban-Style Black Bean Soup, 260
    Duck Breast Pastrami, 286–288
    Grilled Corn and Kale Salad,
        214–216
    Homemade Hot Sauce, 92
    IPA Braised Cheshire Pork Shank,
        198–200
    Milk Braised Ossobuco, 330–332
    Olive Oil Braised Octopus, 314–316
    Paupiettes of Dover Sole, 278–280
    Roasted Sweet Potato with Lentils
        and Roasted Mushrooms,
        302–304
    Seared Venison Chop and Raviolo,
        326–329
    Thai Lobster Bisque en Croûte,
        310–312
    Vichyssoise, 158–160
    White Asparagus with Morel
        Mushrooms and Buttermilk
        Dressing, 172–174
beans
    black
        Chorizo Egg and Cheese
            Empanada, 130–132

Cuban-Style Black Bean Soup,
    260
cannellini
    Ricotta Zeppole, 176–178
fava
    Crab Cakes with Spinach-Ramp
        Purée, 184–186
Beaver Kill Trout, 322–324
beef
    Certified Angus, 137
        BLACKBARN Burger, 134–136
    steaks
        BLACKBARN Tomahawk with
            Herb Butter, 240–242
    ribs
        Eight-Hour Barbecue Beef Ribs,
            282
beer
    Belgian ale
        IPA Braised Cheshire Pork Shank,
            198–200
    IPA
        IPA Braised Cheshire Pork Shank,
            198–200
    stout
        IPA Braised Cheshire Pork Shank,
            198–200
Beetroot Juice, 84
Bigeye Tuna Tartare, 220–222
BLACKBARN Barbecue Sauce, 138
BLACKBARN Burger, 134–136
BLACKBARN Tomahawk with Herb
    Butter, 240–242
blackberries
    Blue Corn "Johnny Cakes," 114
    Summer Berry Zabaglione, 252
Black Mission Fig Pizza, 256–258
Black Winter Truffle Gnocchi, 336–
    338
Bloody Mary, 90
blueberries
    Blue Corn "Johnny Cakes," 114
    Pavlova with Summer Fruit, 248–250
    Summer Berry Zabaglione, 252
Blue Corn "Johnny Cakes," 114
Blushing Basil, 152
Bone Marrow with Manila Clams and
    Shallot Reduction, 192–194
bourbon
    Barnyard Tea, 150
brandy
    BLACKBARN Barbecue Sauce, 138

349   /   BLACKBARN

Corn Flake Crusted French Toast, 122

Thai Lobster Bisque en Croûte, 310–312

Branzino, 39

Roasted Branzino, 224–226

bread

Avocado Toast, 108

Corn Flake Crusted French Toast, 122–124

Maine Lobster Roll, 116–118

Mushroom Toast, 164–166

Roasted Peaches, 245

Rum Butterscotch Bread Pudding, 340–342

breadcrumbs

panko

Bone Marrow with Manila Clams and Shallot Reduction, 192–194

Crab Cakes with Spinach-Ramp Purée, 184–186

Herb-Crusted Atlantic Cod, 318–320

Sautéed Zucchini, 244

bread pudding

Rum Butterscotch Bread Pudding, 340–342

broccoli

Beaver Kill Trout, 322–324

Brussels sprouts

Chestnut Gnocchi, 306–309

Roasted Brussels Sprouts, 334

buttermilk

White Asparagus with Morel Mushrooms and Buttermilk Dressing, 172–174

Butternut Squash Ravioli, 268–270

Butter Poached Maine Lobster with Fresh Pea Soup, 224

butterscotch chips

Rum Butterscotch Bread Pudding, 340–342

C

cake

Frosted Root Carrot Cake, 344

Pumpkin Cheesecake, 296–298

capers

Olive Oil Braised Octopus, 314–316

Caramelized Croissant, 100

cardamom

Curried Cauliflower Steaks, 264–265

Orange Cardamom Cinnamon Buns, 102–104

carrot

colored

Beaver Kill Trout, 322–324

Cuban-Style Black Bean Soup, 260

Frosted Root Carrot Cake, 344

IPA Braised Cheshire Pork Shank, 198–200

Lamb Two Ways with Stuffed Zucchini Flower, 196

Milk Braised Ossobuco, 330–332

Olive Oil Braised Octopus, 314–316

Roasted Branzino, 224–226

Roasted Sweet Potato with Lentils and Roasted Mushrooms, 302–304

Seared Venison Chop and Raviolo, 326–329

Carrot Mixer, 84

carrots

Roasted Heirloom Carrots with English Pea Hummus, 180

Vichyssoise, 158–160

White Asparagus with Morel Mushrooms and Buttermilk Dressing, 172–174

cauliflower

Curried Cauliflower Steaks, 264–265

caviar, 161

paddlefish, 40

Live Day Boat Scallop Crudo, 272

Paupiettes of Dover Sole, 278–280

Siberian Osetra

Vichyssoise, 158–160

cayenne

BLACKBARN Burger, 134–136

celery

Bloody Mary, 90

Crab Cakes with Spinach-Ramp Purée, 184–186

Cuban-Style Black Bean Soup, 260

Green Juice, 84

Milk Braised Ossobuco, 330–332

Paupiettes of Dover Sole, 278–280

Vichyssoise, 158–160

White Asparagus with Morel Mushrooms and Buttermilk Dressing, 172–174

celery root

Seared Venison Chop and Raviolo, 326–329

celery salt

Bloody Mary, 90

champagne

Pavlova with Summer Fruit, 248–250

Summer Berry Zabaglione, 252

chard, Swiss

Butternut Squash Ravioli, 268–270

Charred Gem Lettuce, 112

cheese

blue

Watermelon Salad, 218

burrata

Roasted Peaches, 245

cheddar

white

Chorizo Egg and Cheese Empanada, 130–132

cotija

Shishito Peppers, 202

cream

Frosted Root Carrot Cake, 344

Pumpkin Cheesecake, 296–298

goat

Roasted Figs and Almond Shortbread, 210

Gruyère

BLACKBARN Burger, 134–136

Gougères, 156

Waffle Croque Madame, 126–128

mascarpone

Chestnut Gnocchi, 306–309

Ricotta Zeppole, 176–178

mozzarella

Black Mission Fig Pizza, 256–258

Parmesan

Black Mission Fig Pizza, 256–258

Black Winter Truffle Gnocchi, 336–338

Butternut Squash Ravioli, 268–270

Chestnut Gnocchi, 306–309

Crisp-Skinned Striped Bass, 274–276

Gougères, 156

Milk Braised Ossobuco, 330–332

Mushroom Toast, 164–166

Pan-Seared Day Boat Scallops, 188–190

Polenta Cake with Ratatouille and Marinated Shrimp, 230–232

Ricotta Zeppole, 176–178
ricotta
Black Winter Truffle Gnocchi,
336–338
Blue Corn "Johnny Cakes," 114
Chestnut Gnocchi, 306–309
Ricotta Zeppole, 176–178
ricotta salata
Avocado Toast, 108
Grilled Corn and Kale Salad,
214–216
taleggio
Mushroom Toast, 164–166
cheesecake
Pumpkin Cheesecake, 296–298
Cheese Fondue
Black Mission Fig Pizza, 256–258
Mushroom Toast, 164–166
Chestnut Gnocchi, 306–309
chestnut powder
Chestnut Gnocchi, 306–309
chicken
Amish, 36
Grilled Amish Chicken with
Chimichurri and Panzanella
Salad, 236–237
wings
Crispy Chicken Wings, 162
chicken stock
Vichyssoise, 158–160
chickpeas
Olive Oil Braised Octopus, 314–
316
chili flakes
Roasted Branzino, 224–226
chili powder
ancho
BLACKBARN Burger, 134–136
chipotle
BLACKBARN Burger, 134–136
chimichurri
Grilled Amish Chicken with
Chimichurri and Panzanella Salad,
236–237
chipotle in adobo
Bloody Mary, 90
Chipotle-Orange Spice Rub
BLACKBARN Tomahawk with Herb
Butter, 240–242
Chestnut Gnocchi, 306–309
Crispy Chicken Wings, 162
Eight-Hour Barbecue Beef Ribs, 282
Roasted Sweet Potato with Lentils
and Roasted Mushrooms,
302–304

chipotle paste
BLACKBARN Barbecue Sauce, 138
chives
Bigeye Tuna Tartare, 220–222
Bone Marrow with Manila Clams
and Shallot Reduction, 192–194
Charred Gem Lettuce, 112
Grilled Amish Chicken with
Chimichurri and Panzanella Salad,
236–237
Herb-Crusted Atlantic Cod, 318–320
Live Day Boat Scallop Crudo, 272
Paupiettes of Dover Sole, 278–
280
Waffle Croque Madame, 126–128
Watermelon Salad, 218
chocolate
dark
Chocolate Soufflé, 206–208
Orange Cardamom Cinnamon
Buns, 102–104
Mexican bittersweet
Chorizo Egg and Cheese
Empanada, 130–132
Chocolate Soufflé, 206–208
Chorizo Egg and Cheese Empanada,
130–132
cider
Apple Cider Doughnuts, 292–294
Roasted Acorn Squash, 290
cilantro
Avocado Toast, 108
Bigeye Tuna Tartare, 220–222
Chorizo Egg and Cheese Empanada,
130–132
Cuban-Style Black Bean Soup, 260
Curried Cauliflower Steaks,
264–265
Maine Lobster Roll, 116–118
cinnamon
Apple Cider Doughnuts, 292–294
Corn Flake Crusted French Toast,
122
Crab Cakes with Spinach-Ramp
Purée, 184–186
Curried Cauliflower Steaks,
264–265
Frosted Root Carrot Cake, 344
Orange Cardamom Cinnamon
Buns, 102–104
Pumpkin Cheesecake, 296–298
Roasted Acorn Squash, 290
cinnamon buns
Orange Cardamom Cinnamon
Buns, 102–104

clam juice
Bone Marrow with Manila Clams
and Shallot Reduction, 192–194
clams
Bone Marrow with Manila Clams
and Shallot Reduction, 192–194
Cloud 9, 148
cloves
Chorizo Egg and Cheese Empanada,
130–132
Duck Breast Pastrami, 286–288
Frosted Root Carrot Cake, 344
Pumpkin Cheesecake, 296–298
cockles
Bone Marrow with Manila Clams
and Shallot Reduction, 192–194
cocktails
Barnyard Tea, 150
Bloody Mary, 90
Blushing Basil, 152
Cloud 9, 148
coconut cream
Cloud 9, 148
coconut milk
Thai Lobster Bisque en Croûte,
310–312
cod
Herb-Crusted Atlantic Cod,
318–320
coffee extract
Caramelized Croissant, 100
cookies
amaretto
Butternut Squash Ravioli,
268–270
gingersnap
Pumpkin Cheesecake, 296–298
coriander
Cuban-Style Black Bean Soup, 260
Curried Cauliflower Steaks,
264–265
Duck Breast Pastrami, 286–288
Roasted Branzino, 224–226
corn
bicolor
Grilled Corn and Kale Salad,
214–216
Crisp-Skinned Striped Bass,
274–276
Corn Flake Crusted French Toast,
122–124
corn flakes
Corn Flake Crusted French Toast,
122
cornmeal, Bloody Butcher, 44

Blue Corn "Johnny Cakes," 114
Crab Cakes with Spinach-Ramp Purée, 184–186
crab meat
  Crab Cakes with Spinach-Ramp Purée, 184–186
cream
  Apple Cider Doughnuts, 292–294
  Black Winter Truffle Gnocchi, 336–338
  Bone Marrow with Manila Clams and Shallot Reduction, 192–194
  Butternut Squash Ravioli, 268–270
  Butter Poached Maine Lobster with Fresh Pea Soup, 224
  Chestnut Gnocchi, 306–309
  Corn Flake Crusted French Toast, 122
  Crisp-Skinned Striped Bass, 274–276
  Paupiettes of Dover Sole, 278–280
  Pavlova with Summer Fruit, 248–250
  Rum Butterscotch Bread Pudding, 340–342
  Seared Venison Chop and Raviolo, 326–329
  Vichyssoise, 158–160
crème fraîche
  White Asparagus with Morel Mushrooms and Buttermilk Dressing, 172–174
Crisp-Skinned Striped Bass, 274–276
Crispy Anna Potatoes, 204
Crispy Chicken Wings, 162
croissant
  Almond Honey Croissant, 96–98
  Caramelized Croissant, 100
croutons
  Grilled Amish Chicken with Chimichurri and Panzanella Salad, 236–237
crudo
  Live Day Boat Scallop Crudo, 272
Cuban-Style Black Bean Soup, 260
cucumbers
  Curried Cauliflower Steaks, 264–265
  Green Juice, 84
  Persian
    Grilled Amish Chicken with Chimichurri and Panzanella Salad, 236–237

White Asparagus with Morel Mushrooms and Buttermilk Dressing, 172–174
cumin
  BLACKBARN Burger, 134–136
  Cuban-Style Black Bean Soup, 260
  Curried Cauliflower Steaks, 264–265
  seeds
    Chorizo Egg and Cheese Empanada, 130–132
Curried Cauliflower Steaks, 264–265
curry paste, red Thai
  Thai Lobster Bisque en Croûte, 310–312
curry powder
  Curried Cauliflower Steaks, 264–265

D
dill
  Beaver Kill Trout, 322–324
  Grilled Amish Chicken with Chimichurri and Panzanella Salad, 236–237
  Roasted Sweet Potato with Lentils and Roasted Mushrooms, 302–304
  Watermelon Salad, 218
dough
  Almond Honey Croissant, 96–98
  Thai Lobster Bisque en Croûte, 310–312
doughnuts
  Apple Cider Doughnuts, 292–294
Dover sole
  Paupiettes of Dover Sole, 278–280
duck, 289
  Duck Breast Pastrami, 286–288
Duck Breast Pastrami, 286–288

E
egg
  Chocolate Soufflé, 206–208
  Chorizo Egg and Cheese Empanada, 130–132
  Gougères, 156
  Summer Berry Zabaglione, 252
egg white
  Blushing Basil, 152
  Chocolate Soufflé, 206–208
  Cloud 9, 148
  Summer Berry Zabaglione, 252
Eight-Hour Barbecue Beef Ribs, 282

empanada
  Chorizo Egg and Cheese Empanada, 130–132

F
fennel bulb
  Paupiettes of Dover Sole, 278–280
  Roasted Branzino, 224–226
  Thai Lobster Bisque en Croûte, 310–312
figs
  Black Mission, 40
    Black Mission Fig Pizza, 256–258
    Roasted Figs and Almond Shortbread, 210
fish bones
  Paupiettes of Dover Sole, 278–280
fish heads
  Paupiettes of Dover Sole, 278–280
Frosted Root Carrot Cake, 344

G
garlic
  BLACKBARN Barbecue Sauce, 138
  BLACKBARN Burger, 134–136
  BLACKBARN Tomahawk with Herb Butter, 240–242
  Bone Marrow with Manila Clams and Shallot Reduction, 192–194
  Butter Poached Maine Lobster with Fresh Pea Soup, 224
  Chestnut Gnocchi, 306–309
  Chorizo Egg and Cheese Empanada, 130–132
  Crisp-Skinned Striped Bass, 274–276
  Crispy Anna Potatoes, 204
  Cuban-Style Black Bean Soup, 260
  Curried Cauliflower Steaks, 264–265
  Grilled Amish Chicken with Chimichurri and Panzanella Salad, 236–237
  Herb-Crusted Atlantic Cod, 318–320
  Homemade Hot Sauce, 92
  IPA Braised Cheshire Pork Shank, 198–200
  Lamb Two Ways with Stuffed Zucchini Flower, 196
  Maine Lobster Roll, 116–118

Milk Braised Ossobuco, 330–332
Olive Oil Braised Octopus, 314–316
Pan-Seared Day Boat Scallops, 188–190
Paupiettes of Dover Sole, 278–280
Polenta Cake with Ratatouille and Marinated Shrimp, 230–232
Ricotta Zeppole, 176–178
Roasted Acorn Squash, 290
Roasted Branzino, 224–226
Roasted Brussels Sprouts, 334
Roasted Heirloom Carrots with English Pea Hummus, 180
Sautéed Zucchini, 244
Seared Venison Chop and Raviolo, 326–329
Thai Lobster Bisque en Croûte, 310–312
Vichyssoise, 158–160
White Asparagus with Morel Mushrooms and Buttermilk Dressing, 172–174

gin
Blushing Basil, 152
ginger
Almond Honey Croissant, 96–98
Beetroot Juice, 84
Green Juice, 84
ground
Pumpkin Cheesecake, 296–298
Roasted Acorn Squash, 290
Thai Lobster Bisque en Croûte, 310–312
gnocchi
Black Winter Truffle Gnocchi, 336–338
Chestnut Gnocchi, 306–309
Gougères, 156
grapes
red
Roasted Heirloom Carrots with English Pea Hummus, 180
Green Goddess Dressing, 112
Grilled Corn and Kale Salad, 214–216
Green Juice, 84
Grilled Amish Chicken with Chimichurri and Panzanella Salad, 236–237
Grilled Corn and Kale Salad, 214–216

H

ham
Waffle Croque Madame, 126–128

hamburger
BLACKBARN Burger, 134–136
heirloom vegetables, 182
Herb-Crusted Atlantic Cod, 318–320
Homemade Hot Sauce, 92
honey, 44
Almond Honey Croissant, 96–98
Beetroot Juice, 84
elderflower
Blue Corn "Johnny Cakes," 114
honeycomb
Blue Corn "Johnny Cakes," 114
horseradish
Bloody Mary, 90
hot sauce, 92
Bloody Mary, 90
Crispy Chicken Wings, 162
IPA Braised Cheshire Pork Shank, 198–200

I

IPA Braised Cheshire Pork Shank, 198–200

J

jalapeño
Avocado Toast, 108
Bigeye Tuna Tartare, 220–222
BLACKBARN Burger, 134–136
Charred Gem Lettuce, 112
Grilled Corn and Kale Salad, 214–216
Olive Oil Braised Octopus, 314–316
jam
fig
Black Mission Fig Pizza, 256–258
Johnny cakes
Blue Corn "Johnny Cakes," 114
juices
Beetroot Juice, 84
Carrot Mixer, 84
Green Juice, 84
juniper berries
Homemade Hot Sauce, 92

K

kale
Green Juice, 84
Grilled Corn and Kale Salad, 214–216

L

labneh, 45
Charred Gem Lettuce, 112

Roasted Sweet Potato with Lentils and Roasted Mushrooms, 302–304
lady fingers
Summer Berry Zabaglione, 252
lamb
ground
Lamb Two Ways with Stuffed Zucchini Flower, 196
rack of
Lamb Two Ways with Stuffed Zucchini Flower, 196
Lamb Two Ways with Stuffed Zucchini Flower, 196
leeks
Vichyssoise, 158–160
lemon
Barnyard Tea, 150
Beetroot Juice, 84
Blushing Basil, 152
Green Juice, 84
Olive Oil Braised Octopus, 314–316
Roasted Branzino, 224–226
Lemon Dressing, 108
Bigeye Tuna Tartare, 220–222
Curried Cauliflower Steaks, 264–265
Mushroom Toast, 164–166
Pan-Seared Day Boat Scallops, 188–190
Roasted Heirloom Carrots with English Pea Hummus, 180
lemongrass
Thai Lobster Bisque en Croûte, 310–312
lemon juice
Almond Honey Croissant, 96–98
Avocado Toast, 108
Barnyard Tea, 150
Beaver Kill Trout, 322–324
Crab Cakes with Spinach-Ramp Purée, 184–186
Curried Cauliflower Steaks, 264–265
Maine Lobster Roll, 116–118
Pavlova with Summer Fruit, 248–250
White Asparagus with Morel Mushrooms and Buttermilk Dressing, 172–174
lemon zest
Bigeye Tuna Tartare, 220–222
Grilled Amish Chicken with Chimichurri and Panzanella Salad, 236–237
Herb-Crusted Atlantic Cod, 318–320

Pavlova with Summer Fruit,
248–250
Roasted Heirloom Carrots with
English Pea Hummus, 180
Summer Berry Zabaglione, 252
lentils
beluga, 40
Roasted Sweet Potato
with Lentils and Roasted
Mushrooms, 302–304
lettuce
arugula
Black Mission Fig Pizza, 256–
258
Bibb
BLACKBARN Burger, 134–136
gem
Charred Gem Lettuce, 112
romaine
Curried Cauliflower Steaks,
264–265
lime juice
Bigeye Tuna Tartare, 220–222
Cloud 9, 148
Cuban-Style Black Bean Soup, 260
Curried Cauliflower Steaks,
264–265
Roasted Heirloom Carrots with
English Pea Hummus, 180
Thai Lobster Bisque en Croûte,
310–312
White Asparagus with Morel
Mushrooms and Buttermilk
Dressing, 172–174
lime zest
Roasted Heirloom Carrots with
English Pea Hummus, 180
White Asparagus with Morel
Mushrooms and Buttermilk
Dressing, 172–174
limoncello, pink
Blushing Basil, 152
Live Day Boat Scallop Crudo, 272
lobster, 119
Butter Poached Maine Lobster with
Fresh Pea Soup, 224
Maine Lobster Roll, 116–118
Thai Lobster Bisque en Croûte,
310–312

M
Maine Lobster Roll, 116–118
maple syrup
Butternut Squash Ravioli, 268–270

Corn Flake Crusted French Toast,
122
Roasted Figs and Almond
Shortbread, 210
mayonnaise
Crab Cakes with Spinach-Ramp
Purée, 184–186
White Asparagus with Morel
Mushrooms and Buttermilk
Dressing, 172–174
Milk Braised Ossobuco, 330–332
mint
Barnyard Tea, 150
Butter Poached Maine Lobster with
Fresh Pea Soup, 224
Charred Gem Lettuce, 112
Crab Cakes with Spinach-Ramp
Purée, 184–186
Grilled Amish Chicken with
Chimichurri and Panzanella Salad,
236–237
Pan-Seared Day Boat Scallops,
188–190
Paupiettes of Dover Sole, 278–
280
Roasted Branzino, 224–226
Roasted Sweet Potato with Lentils
and Roasted Mushrooms,
302–304
Watermelon Salad, 218
molasses
Pumpkin Cheesecake, 296–298
Rum Butterscotch Bread Pudding,
340–342
mole sauce
Chorizo Egg and Cheese Empanada,
130–132
mostarda
Butternut Squash Ravioli, 268–270
mushrooms, 167
chanterelle
Crisp-Skinned Striped Bass,
274–276
Herb-Crusted Atlantic Cod,
318–320
Milk Braised Ossobuco, 330–332
morel
White Asparagus with Morel
Mushrooms and Buttermilk
Dressing, 172–174
Roasted Sweet Potato with Lentils
and Roasted Mushrooms,
302–304
Mushroom Toast, 164–166

mustard
Dijon
Crab Cakes with Spinach-Ramp
Purée, 184–186
Live Day Boat Scallop Crudo, 272
mustard seed
Duck Breast Pastrami, 286–288

N
nutmeg
Apple Cider Doughnuts, 292–294
Butternut Squash Ravioli, 268–270
Curried Cauliflower Steaks,
264–265
Duck Breast Pastrami, 286–288
Frosted Root Carrot Cake, 344
Gougères, 156
Pumpkin Cheesecake, 296–298
Roasted Acorn Squash, 290
Seared Venison Chop and Raviolo,
326–329
Vichyssoise, 158–160
Waffle Croque Madame, 126–128

O
octopus
Olive Oil Braised Octopus, 314–316
Old Bay Seasoning
Crab Cakes with Spinach-Ramp
Purée, 184–186
Olive Oil Braised Octopus, 314–316
olives
Castelvetrano
Roasted Branzino, 224–226
Queen
Olive Oil Braised Octopus,
314–316
onions
Bermuda
Watermelon Salad, 218
BLACKBARN Burger, 134–136
IPA Braised Cheshire Pork Shank,
198–200
red
Avocado Toast, 108
Bigeye Tuna Tartare, 220–222
Chorizo Egg and Cheese
Empanada, 130–132
Curried Cauliflower Steaks,
264–265
Grilled Amish Chicken with
Chimichurri and Panzanella
Salad, 236–237
Polenta Cake with Ratatouille and
Marinated Shrimp, 230–232

354   /   BLACKBARN

Thai Lobster Bisque en Croûte, 310–312
Spanish, 47
BLACKBARN Barbecue Sauce, 138
Crisp-Skinned Striped Bass, 274–276
Cuban-Style Black Bean Soup, 260
Grilled Corn and Kale Salad, 214–216
Homemade Hot Sauce, 92
IPA Braised Cheshire Pork Shank, 198–200
Olive Oil Braised Octopus, 314–316
Pan-Seared Day Boat Scallops, 188–190
Paupiettes of Dover Sole, 278–280
Roasted Sweet Potato with Lentils and Roasted Mushrooms, 302–304
Seared Venison Chop and Raviolo, 326–329
Vichyssoise, 158–160
White Asparagus with Morel Mushrooms and Buttermilk Dressing, 172–174
white
Chorizo Egg and Cheese Empanada, 130–132
IPA Braised Cheshire Pork Shank, 198–200
yellow
Milk Braised Ossobuco, 330–332
Vichyssoise, 158–160
Orange Cardamom Cinnamon Buns, 102–104
orange juice
Charred Gem Lettuce, 112
orange peel
BLACKBARN Burger, 134–136
oranges
blood
Beaver Kill Trout, 322–324
Carrot Mixer, 84
orange zest
BLACKBARN Burger, 134–136
blood
Frosted Root Carrot Cake, 344
Corn Flake Crusted French Toast, 122
Orange Cardamom Cinnamon Buns, 102–104
Roasted Branzino, 224–226

oregano
BLACKBARN Barbecue Sauce, 138
Grilled Amish Chicken with Chimichurri and Panzanella Salad, 236–237
Roasted Sweet Potato with Lentils and Roasted Mushrooms, 302–304

P

pancetta
Milk Braised Ossobuco, 330–332
Pan-Seared Day Boat Scallops, 188–190
Pan-Seared Day Boat Scallops, 188–190
paprika
BLACKBARN Burger, 134–136
Bloody Mary, 90
Butternut Squash Ravioli, 268–270
smoked
Beaver Kill Trout, 322–324
BLACKBARN Barbecue Sauce, 138
BLACKBARN Burger, 134–136
White Asparagus with Morel Mushrooms and Buttermilk Dressing, 172–174
parsley, 278–280
Beaver Kill Trout, 322–324
BLACKBARN Tomahawk with Herb Butter, 240–242
Bone Marrow with Manila Clams and Shallot Reduction, 192–194
Cuban-Style Black Bean Soup, 260
Grilled Amish Chicken with Chimichurri and Panzanella Salad, 236–237
Herb-Crusted Atlantic Cod, 318–320
Maine Lobster Roll, 116–118
Milk Braised Ossobuco, 330–332
Mushroom Toast, 164–166
Olive Oil Braised Octopus, 314–316
Roasted Branzino, 224–226
Roasted Sweet Potato with Lentils and Roasted Mushrooms, 302–304
Vichyssoise, 158–160
Watermelon Salad, 218
parsnips
White Asparagus with Morel Mushrooms and Buttermilk Dressing, 172–174
passion fruit juice
Carrot Mixer, 84

pasta
Butternut Squash Ravioli, 268–270
Seared Venison Chop and Raviolo, 326–329
pastrami
Duck Breast Pastrami, 286–288
pastries
Almond Honey Croissant, 96–98
Caramelized Croissant, 100
Orange Cardamom Cinnamon Buns, 102–104
Paupiettes of Dover Sole, 278–280
Pavlova with Summer Fruit, 248–250
peaches
Roasted Peaches, 245
peanuts
Chorizo Egg and Cheese Empanada, 130–132
pears
Almond Honey Croissant, 96–98
peas
English
Butter Poached Maine Lobster with Fresh Pea Soup, 224
Pan-Seared Day Boat Scallops, 188–190
Roasted Heirloom Carrots with English Pea Hummus, 180
pea shoots
Roasted Peaches, 245
pea tendrils
Pan-Seared Day Boat Scallops, 188–190
peppers
ancho
Chorizo Egg and Cheese Empanada, 130–132
Homemade Hot Sauce, 92
bell
red
Chorizo Egg and Cheese Empanada, 130–132
Cuban-Style Black Bean Soup, 260
Homemade Hot Sauce, 92
Olive Oil Braised Octopus, 314–316
Polenta Cake with Ratatouille and Marinated Shrimp, 230–232
yellow
Chorizo Egg and Cheese Empanada, 130–132

guajillo
Chorizo Egg and Cheese
Empanada, 130–132
Homemade Hot Sauce, 92
pasilla
Chorizo Egg and Cheese
Empanada, 130–132
shishito, 45, 202
sweet cherry
Homemade Hot Sauce, 92
Thai chilis
Roasted Peaches, 245
pickle
Bloody Mary, 90
Pico de Gallo
Cuban-Style Black Bean Soup, 260
Shishito Peppers, 202
pineapple
Beetroot Juice, 84
Carrot Mixer, 84
pineapple juice
Cloud 9, 148
pine nuts
Curried Cauliflower Steaks,
264–265
Olive Oil Braised Octopus, 314–316
Ricotta Zeppole, 176–178
pistachios
Crab Cakes with Spinach-Ramp
Purée, 184–186
Frosted Root Carrot Cake, 344
pizza, 259
Black Mission Fig Pizza, 256–258
polenta
Milk Braised Ossobuco, 330–332
Polenta Cake with Ratatouille and
Marinated Shrimp, 230–232
pomegranate seeds
Beaver Kill Trout, 322–324
Chestnut Gnocchi, 306–309
Roasted Acorn Squash, 290
pork
heritage Cheshire, 39–40
IPA Braised Cheshire Pork Shank,
198–200
spicy coppa
Black Mission Fig Pizza, 256–
258
potato
Chestnut Gnocchi, 306–309
Chorizo Egg and Cheese Empanada,
130–132
Crispy Anna Potatoes, 204
fingerling
Beaver Kill Trout, 322–324

Herb-Crusted Atlantic Cod,
318–320
Seared Venison Chop and Raviolo,
326–329
sweet
Roasted Sweet Potato
with Lentils and Roasted
Mushrooms, 302–304
Vichyssoise, 158–160
Yukon
Roasted Branzino, 224–226
produce, Hudson Valley, 44
prosecco
Summer Berry Zabaglione, 252
pudding
Rum Butterscotch Bread Pudding,
340–342
Pumpkin Cheesecake, 296–298
pumpkin seeds
Butternut Squash Ravioli, 268–270

Q
queso fresco
Chorizo Egg and Cheese Empanada,
130–132

R
radicchio
Curried Cauliflower Steaks,
264–265
Grilled Corn and Kale Salad,
214–216
radishes
French breakfast
Crab Cakes with Spinach-Ramp
Purée, 184–186
raisins
golden
Chorizo Egg and Cheese
Empanada, 130–132
Curried Cauliflower Steaks,
264–265
Rum Butterscotch Bread
Pudding, 340–342
Seared Venison Chop and Raviolo,
326–329
ramps
Crab Cakes with Spinach-Ramp
Purée, 184–186
raspberries
Blue Corn "Johnny Cakes," 114
Pavlova with Summer Fruit,
248–250
Summer Berry Zabaglione, 252
ratatouille, 234

Polenta Cake with Ratatouille and
Marinated Shrimp, 230–232
ravioli
Butternut Squash Ravioli, 268–270
Seared Venison Chop and Raviolo,
326–329
red pepper flakes
Crab Cakes with Spinach-Ramp
Purée, 184–186
Maine Lobster Roll, 116–118
Thai Lobster Bisque en Croûte,
310–312
ribs
Eight-Hour Barbecue Beef Ribs,
282
rice
Carnaroli
Crisp-Skinned Striped Bass,
274–276
Pan-Seared Day Boat Scallops,
188–190
Ricotta Zeppole, 176–178
Roasted Acorn Squash, 290
Roasted Branzino, 224–226
Roasted Brussels Sprouts, 334
Roasted Figs and Almond Shortbread,
210
Roasted Garlic Cloves
BLACKBARN Tomahawk with Herb
Butter, 240–242
Roasted Heirloom Carrots with
English Pea Hummus, 180
Roasted Peaches, 245
Roasted Sweet Potato with Lentils and
Roasted Mushrooms, 302–304
roe
salmon
Paupiettes of Dover Sole,
278–280
trout
Live Day Boat Scallop Crudo,
272
rosemary
BLACKBARN Tomahawk with Herb
Butter, 240–242
Crispy Anna Potatoes, 204
Cuban-Style Black Bean Soup, 260
Lamb Two Ways with Stuffed
Zucchini Flower, 196
Milk Braised Ossobuco, 330–332
Ricotta Zeppole, 176–178
Roasted Acorn Squash, 290
Roasted Branzino, 224–226
Roasted Peaches, 245
Sautéed Zucchini, 244

Seared Venison Chop and Raviolo, 326–329
rum
  white
    Cloud 9, 148
Rum Butterscotch Bread Pudding, 340–342

S

sage
  BLACKBARN Tomahawk with Herb Butter, 240–242
  Butternut Squash Ravioli, 268–270
  Roasted Acorn Squash, 290
sage leaves
  Seared Venison Chop and Raviolo, 326–329
salad
  Grilled Amish Chicken with Chimichurri and Panzanella Salad, 236–237
  Grilled Corn and Kale Salad, 214–216
  Watermelon Salad, 218
salmon roe
  Paupiettes of Dover Sole, 278–280
sausage
  chorizo
    Chorizo Egg and Cheese Empanada, 130–132
Sautéed Zucchini, 244
scallops, Atlantic Day Boat, 36, 191
  Live Day Boat Scallop Crudo, 272
  Pan-Seared Day Boat Scallops, 188–190
sea beans, 45
  Paupiettes of Dover Sole, 278–280
Seared Venison Chop and Raviolo, 326–329
sesame oil
  Roasted Heirloom Carrots with English Pea Hummus, 180
sesame seeds
  Chorizo Egg and Cheese Empanada, 130–132
shallots
  Bone Marrow with Manila Clams and Shallot Reduction, 192–194
  Butternut Squash Ravioli, 268–270
  Butter Poached Maine Lobster with Fresh Pea Soup, 224
  Crab Cakes with Spinach-Ramp Purée, 184–186

Crisp-Skinned Striped Bass, 274–276
Duck Breast Pastrami, 286–288
Herb-Crusted Atlantic Cod, 318–320
Maine Lobster Roll, 116–118
Mushroom Toast, 164–166
Olive Oil Braised Octopus, 314–316
Pan-Seared Day Boat Scallops, 188–190
Paupiettes of Dover Sole, 278–280
Roasted Sweet Potato with Lentils and Roasted Mushrooms, 302–304
Sautéed Zucchini, 244
White Asparagus with Morel Mushrooms and Buttermilk Dressing, 172–174
shishito peppers, 45, 202
shrimp
  Paupiettes of Dover Sole, 278–280
  Polenta Cake with Ratatouille and Marinated Shrimp, 230–232
sofrito
  Chorizo Egg and Cheese Empanada, 130–132
sole
  Paupiettes of Dover Sole, 278–280
soup
  Butter Poached Maine Lobster with Fresh Pea Soup, 224
  Cuban-Style Black Bean Soup, 260
spicy coppa
  Black Mission Fig Pizza, 256–258
spinach
  baby
    Crab Cakes with Spinach-Ramp Purée, 184–186
squash
  acorn
    Roasted Acorn Squash, 290
  butternut
    Butternut Squash Ravioli, 268–270
star anise
  Chorizo Egg and Cheese Empanada, 130–132
  Homemade Hot Sauce, 92
  Roasted Acorn Squash, 290
  Roasted Branzino, 224–226
strawberries
  Blue Corn "Johnny Cakes," 114

Pavlova with Summer Fruit, 248–250
Summer Berry Zabaglione, 252
striped bass
  Crisp-Skinned Striped Bass, 274–276
  East Coast, 39
Summer Berry Zabaglione, 252
syrup, simple
  Blushing Basil, 152

T

tahini
  Olive Oil Braised Octopus, 314–316
  Roasted Heirloom Carrots with English Pea Hummus, 180
tarragon
  Charred Gem Lettuce, 112
  Grilled Amish Chicken with Chimichurri and Panzanella Salad, 236–237
  Herb-Crusted Atlantic Cod, 318–320
  Roasted Branzino, 224–226
tea
  black
    Barnyard Tea, 150
Thai Lobster Bisque en Croûte, 310–312
thyme
  BLACKBARN Barbecue Sauce, 138
  BLACKBARN Tomahawk with Herb Butter, 240–242
  Bone Marrow with Manila Clams and Shallot Reduction, 192–194
  Butter Poached Maine Lobster with Fresh Pea Soup, 224
  Chestnut Gnocchi, 306–309
  Crisp-Skinned Striped Bass, 274–276
  Crispy Anna Potatoes, 204
  Cuban-Style Black Bean Soup, 260
  Curried Cauliflower Steaks, 264–265
  Duck Breast Pastrami, 286–288
  Grilled Amish Chicken with Chimichurri and Panzanella Salad, 236–237
  Grilled Corn and Kale Salad, 214–216
  Herb-Crusted Atlantic Cod, 318–320
  Homemade Hot Sauce, 92

IPA Braised Cheshire Pork Shank, 198–200
Lamb Two Ways with Stuffed Zucchini Flower, 196
Maine Lobster Roll, 116–118
Milk Braised Ossobuco, 330–332
Mushroom Toast, 164–166
Olive Oil Braised Octopus, 314–316
Pan-Seared Day Boat Scallops, 188–190
Paupiettes of Dover Sole, 278–280
Pavlova with Summer Fruit, 248–250
Polenta Cake with Ratatouille and Marinated Shrimp, 230–232
Roasted Branzino, 224–226
Roasted Brussels Sprouts, 334
Roasted Heirloom Carrots with English Pea Hummus, 180
Roasted Sweet Potato with Lentils and Roasted Mushrooms, 302–304
Sautéed Zucchini, 244
Seared Venison Chop and Raviolo, 326–329
Thai Lobster Bisque en Croûte, 310–312
Vichyssoise, 158–160
White Asparagus with Morel Mushrooms and Buttermilk Dressing, 172–174
toast
Avocado Toast, 108
Corn Flake Crusted French Toast, 122–124
Mushroom Toast, 164–166
tomatillos
IPA Braised Cheshire Pork Shank, 198–200
tomatoes
Bigeye Tuna Tartare, 220–222
cherry
Grilled Amish Chicken with Chimichurri and Panzanella Salad, 236–237
Grilled Corn and Kale Salad, 214–216
Lamb Two Ways with Stuffed Zucchini Flower, 196
Ricotta Zeppole, 176–178
grape
Curried Cauliflower Steaks, 264–265

plum
BLACKBARN Burger, 134–136
cherry
Maine Lobster Roll, 116–118
Chorizo Egg and Cheese Empanada, 130–132
Polenta Cake with Ratatouille and Marinated Shrimp, 230–232
tomato juice
Bloody Mary, 90
Grilled Amish Chicken with Chimichurri and Panzanella Salad, 236–237
tomato paste
BLACKBARN Barbecue Sauce, 138
Bloody Mary, 90
Thai Lobster Bisque en Croûte, 310–312
tortilla
corn
Bigeye Tuna Tartare, 220–222
Chorizo Egg and Cheese Empanada, 130–132
Cuban-Style Black Bean Soup, 260
trout, 324
Beaver Kill Trout, 322–324
trout roe
Live Day Boat Scallop Crudo, 272
truffle
black winter
Black Winter Truffle Gnocchi, 336–338
truffle oil
Black Mission Fig Pizza, 256–258
truffles
black winter, 40–44
tuna
bigeye, 36, 39
Bigeye Tuna Tartare, 220–222
turnips
Chestnut Gnocchi, 306–309

V

vegetables, heirloom, 182
venison
Seared Venison Chop and Raviolo, 326–329
Vichyssoise, 158–160
vinegar
apple balsamic
Roasted Figs and Almond Shortbread, 210

apple cider
White Asparagus with Morel Mushrooms and Buttermilk Dressing, 172–174
balsamic
Black Mission Fig Pizza, 256–258
Moscatel, 45
Duck Breast Pastrami, 286–288
Grilled Amish Chicken with Chimichurri and Panzanella Salad, 236–237
Live Day Boat Scallop Crudo, 272
red wine
Crab Cakes with Spinach-Ramp Purée, 184–186
Grilled Amish Chicken with Chimichurri and Panzanella Salad, 236–237
Maine Lobster Roll, 116–118
Saba
Roasted Peaches, 245
sherry
BLACKBARN Barbecue Sauce, 138
Crisp-Skinned Striped Bass, 274–276
Grilled Amish Chicken with Chimichurri and Panzanella Salad, 236–237
Herb-Crusted Atlantic Cod, 318–320
Polenta Cake with Ratatouille and Marinated Shrimp, 230–232
Roasted Sweet Potato with Lentils and Roasted Mushrooms, 302–304
White Asparagus with Morel Mushrooms and Buttermilk Dressing, 172–174
white wine
Bone Marrow with Manila Clams and Shallot Reduction, 192–194
Curried Cauliflower Steaks, 264–265
Grilled Corn and Kale Salad, 214–216
Homemade Hot Sauce, 92
Live Day Boat Scallop Crudo, 272
Watermelon Salad, 218
vodka
Bloody Mary, 90

W

Waffle Croque Madame, 126–128
walnuts
  Ricotta Zeppole, 176–178
watercress
  Mushroom Toast, 164–166
  Roasted Heirloom Carrots with
    English Pea Hummus, 180
Watermelon Salad, 218
White Asparagus with Morel
  Mushrooms and Buttermilk
  Dressing, 172–174
wine
  champagne
    Pavlova with Summer Fruit,
      248–250
    Summer Berry Zabaglione, 252
  Pan-Seared Day Boat Scallops,
    188–190
  prosecco
    Summer Berry Zabaglione, 252
  red
    Olive Oil Braised Octopus,
      314–316
    Seared Venison Chop and
      Raviolo, 326–329
  sweet
    Pavlova with Summer Fruit,
      248–250
  white
    Bone Marrow with Manila
      Clams and Shallot Reduction,
      192–194
    Butter Poached Maine Lobster
      with Fresh Pea Soup, 224
    Crisp-Skinned Striped Bass,
      274–276
    Duck Breast Pastrami, 286–288
    Milk Braised Ossobuco, 330–
      332
    Paupiettes of Dover Sole,
      278–280
  white Bordeaux
    Roasted Peaches, 245
Worcestershire sauce
  Bloody Mary, 90

Y

yogurt
  Greek
    Curried Cauliflower Steaks,
      264–265

Roasted Sweet Potato with Lentils
  and Roasted Mushrooms,
  302–304

Z

Za'atar spice, 47
  Roasted Heirloom Carrots with
    English Pea Hummus, 108
  Roasted Sweet Potato with Lentils
    and Roasted Mushrooms,
    302–304
zabaglione
  Summer Berry Zabaglione, 252
zucchini
  Polenta Cake with Ratatouille and
    Marinated Shrimp, 230–232
  Sautéed Zucchini, 244
zucchini flowers
  Lamb Two Ways with Stuffed
    Zucchini Flower, 196